Strong Walk

Strong Walk

Becoming a Lifestyle Spiritual Warrior

Randy Sprinkle

NEW HOPE
PUBLISHERS

Birmingham, Alabama

New Hope® Publishers
P. O. Box 12065
Birmingham, AL 35202-2065
www.newhopepublishers.com

Library of Congress Cataloging-in-Publication Data

Sprinkle, Randy, 1949-

 Strong walk : becoming a lifestyle spiritual warrior : "give the enemy no opportunity" (1 Timothy 5:14 NIV) / Randy Sprinkle.

   p. cm.

 ISBN-13: 978-1-59669-034-9 (softcover)

 1. Spiritual warfare. I. Title.

 BV4509.5.S72 2006

 235'.4—dc22

2006018133

ISBN-10: 1-59669-034-8

ISBN-13: 978-1-59669-034-9

N064149 • 0107 • 4M1

To the warriors
who set a prayer perimeter
around me and labored
in intercession
that this book might
be useful
in His hands
and in yours.

"Give the enemy no opportunity"
(1 Timothy 5:14 NIV).

Table of Contents

Introduction

How excited the father was when the news came that the new baby was a boy. He had so wanted a son! Now he had one. The father doted on his son, especially as the years advanced and the couple had no more children.

Then came that horrible day that still haunted his dreams. From the first incident when the boy was picked up like a helpless puppy and thrown around, the father knew: his son had been seized by a demon. Many other incidents and injuries followed: burns, cuts, bruises, and near-drownings.

While the son's sad story spread from house to house, another story also spread. A stranger was in the region doing strange things, marvelous things. He, too, was under some influence, but everything He did was to help people, not hurt them. He reminded the people of John the Baptist, recently beheaded by the king. Maybe John had come back to life. Others insisted he was Elijah reincarnate, or at least one of the other great prophets of old. Regardless of who he was, this man was good, very good.

The father immediately took his son and began to search for the stranger. As he followed up false leads, he tried to not to lose his flicker of hope. After all, he had been asking his God for years to help. Maybe this was the answer. Finally, he got a credible lead—but when he arrived at the location, he cried. The man wasn't there. Then someone nearby suggested His "right-hand men" could help. Some of them were nearby. Taking his son to them, he asked. They seemed sympathetic but turned out to be just pathetic. They couldn't do anything.

As the father sat on his heels in the dust, unsure what path to take, he heard a growing murmur. Looking up, the father saw, coming down the hillside, the great man. Jumping up, the father began to shout. Unbelievably, the man heard him and began to come his way. When He drew near He invited, "Bring your son here to Me."

But before the father could get to him, the demon, sensing the eminent loss of his prize, slammed the boy to the ground, scattering the crowd in panic, and sending the poor boy into convulsions. From a safe distance, the bystanders witnessed something they could never stop retelling for the rest of their lives. In just a moment, and with just a word, the demon became the one convulsing in pain as it fled the boy and the scene. Then lifting the lad up, the stranger gave him back to his father, freed and restored (Luke 9:37–42; Matthew 17:14–18; Mark 9:14–27).

The church had shown such promise when first it was established on the edge of the growing town. The members' sacrifice and hard work helped it flourish. But looking back over the decades, older members observed, "Every time our church seemed to finally be growing and going somewhere, something happened to send it reeling backwards. There was that affair between two leaders. Then the time that little group just would not stop spreading rumors about the pastor. He finally left. And, yes, gossip always seemed to be a problem. Could that have had any connection to the lack of trust and love that have always characterized our church? No, it had to be the pastors. Remember that one who showed such promise? He ended up setting one side of the congregation against the other and finally took his group off to start their own church.

"Our church really looks good from the street, but it doesn't have a very good reputation in town. Looking back, it seems the enemy was more pleased with what went on in our church than the Lord was."

The job offer from a large Christian organization was a dream come true. After years in a secular firm with its good pay but crude and cutthroat environment, the Christian virtues in her new workplace would, she felt, more than compensate for the lower pay. After a year, though, she returned to the corporate world. She was still sorting through her experience; but the jealousy, scheming, criticism, disputes, complaints, and general absence of love were too familiar. Pretense was far more important than purity. The Holy Spirit sure wasn't the guiding spirit.

Missionary leaders from across a vast, unevangelized area of the world gathered for a week of prayer and strategic training in a distant nation where they thought they would be safe. At the week's midpoint, deep in the night, one of the teachers was suddenly attacked, choked by a horrifying demon. Despite an intense struggle the demon was gaining the upper hand. Then, with all-out effort, the teacher gasped out one word, the name, "Jesus." Then again, "Jesus," And again, "Jesus." With each declaration the demon weakened, and in a matter of seconds released his suffocating grip and fled into the folds of darkness.

"Sixty years after Allied soldiers liberated the Nazi death camps, the world stands silent in the face of another holocaust—one so horrifying that U.N. officials call it 'one of the worst human-rights crises of the past century.'

"The perpetrators commit atrocities with such malevolence that even the most irreligious people familiar with their acts describe them as 'unrestrained evil.' The targets of the butchery are children. They rape, mutilate, and kill them with a rapaciousness that staggers the imagination. Worse, they compel children to kill one another and their own families, fighting as 'soldiers' in an armed force deliberately composed of children.

"Perhaps the greatest atrocity is teaching these children that they spread this carnage by the power of the Holy Spirit to purify the 'unrepentant,' twisting Christianity into a religion of horror to their victims. It is spiritual warfare at its very worst, and it could not be more satanic."

Christianity Today, January 2006
(Referring to the so-called Lord's Resistance Army in Uganda)

It's been said, "The Christian life is the exciting process of trying to maintain your balance." Probably nowhere is this more true than in the area of spiritual warfare, especially when we recognize and accept the fact that all of life is lived in a war zone.

That we live in a contrary world infiltrated by hostile forces and that our pilgrimage through it is one of struggle, difficulty, and, at times even vicious, inexplicable attack is generally accepted by Christians. There are three ways to chart a path through this territory: complicity, compromise, or commitment. For believers the first is not an option. Complicity with the enemy can bring short-term benefit. Our awful enemy *will* do good for us—but at a high price. Inherently we know this, so far more often the course of choice is the second, compromise. Be tolerant, be agreeable, work out a way to get along with the world while trying to stay on the path toward a better one to come. It's OK to be a Christian at home, at church, but when you go out, go underground. While this approach seems better, it isn't. Compromise is just a seemingly more palatable form of complicity. The end result of both is the same: distress and defeat.

This book is about the only real, but too rarely accepted choice for Christians: commitment, a commitment to follow Jesus each day and to follow Him His way. Yet the best choice doesn't seem best and it often doesn't feel best. More, not less, struggle seems to characterize this choice. Only as we learn the way and stay the course do we begin to see it's the only way and thus the only way of victory. It, like so much of the true Christian life, contains many paradoxes. The first paradox is this:

The journey forward begins with a step backwards.

The Way Is a Walk

God's original design for us was one of ongoing, intimate fellowship with Him. The Bible describes this as a walk and reveals that in the Garden of Eden, before the Fall, God would come in the cool of the day and walk with Adam and Eve. Their fellowship together was transparent and uninhibited. Despite the presence of an enemy, life was not just good, it was glorious. But the enemy was not about to leave things as they were. He loathed the people and God and he had a plan. That plan was to separate from God that which was most precious to Him, the very ones He loved to be with.

His effort was successful. Eve was unwittingly drawn into a conversation with the devil that resulted in both Eve and her husband giving in to desire for what was off-limits with an act they thought would elevate them to God level. By the time they learned that the enemy's promise was actually a trap, it was too late. They had already lost everything.

This wasn't the end of the story. The God who loved them was already planning to love them back to Himself, but He had a dilemma. The couple had ordered and eaten but now they couldn't pay their check. Even though they didn't yet realize it, their only hope was for someone else to pick up the tab. And that's exactly what God intended to do.

He knew that there was only One who could settle their account. That One was His own Son, Jesus. He, having the same all-knowing attribute that His Father had, knew the cost; and knowing, still was willing. When all was ready, God sent Jesus on the mission. The cost was as expected, His very life, and He paid it in full. A way was opened for God to be with His beloved again. What anticipation! The invitation was issued. The whole human race could come. And their journey would begin with a step backwards.

Those who say that you can never go home again don't know what they're talking about. When it comes to God, you can come back. You can come home. And one by one they began to. That first step back, back toward home, was the key. It opened their eyes. They thought Jesus had *made* a way back for them. When they turned, they discovered that He *was* that way. And not only was He the way back, He was both guide and outfitter for the journey. He knew the way and He would lead. He knew what was needed for safe passage and He'd already gathered the equipment and was ready to issue it. With that turning around from the self-determined way that they had been walking and moving now in His intended direction, another paradox surfaced. By turning back, they realized they weren't back. They were back as part of the family, back in the loving relationship; but there was still a long walk back to the level of intimate, uninhibited relationship that they had been created for in the beginning. But not to worry. Jesus would take care of that as well. He simply said, "You just follow Me."

As they followed Him, other things became clear. While their relationship with God was restored, the world wasn't. It was not only still really messed up, it was downright dangerous.

The enemy that was there at the beginning was still around with the same insidious intent: to keep them from living the life for which they had been created.

If all of that weren't enough, while the real essence of each person, the spirit of the woman or man, was moving in the right direction, the "flesh" of the person wasn't. It was pulling in the opposite direction, still lined up with the purposes of the enemy. The walk back was looking more like a struggle back—an inner struggle in an atmosphere of struggle with an enemy who was determined to harass and destroy. This wasn't looking good until the traveler glanced again to Jesus. Then the journey not only looked desirable, it looked doable. What seemed impossible (and actually is) didn't seem impossible anymore (and actually isn't) when seen in context, in Jesus context. He makes the difference because He is the difference.

A Personal Question

Could I ask you a personal question? You have read this far because you have some interest in, or curiosity about, spiritual warfare. You have experienced the pain and hurt that come from our enemy (even though you may not have realized that he even existed). Victory and joy in life are genuine possibilities but they are dependent on one decision: the decision to leave behind the self-directed life and turn and become a follower of Jesus. Have *you* done that?

If you haven't, He says to you today, "*Come to Me, all who are weary and heavy-laden, and I will give you rest*" (Matthew 11:28). He will. No need to hurt alone anymore. Jesus loves you.

And if you have already begun to follow Jesus, pause and thank Him again for loving you enough to pay your debt by giving His life for yours. (I'll wait for you while you do that.)

Now, with new gratitude and fresh commitment to follow Him, let's begin a journey into the way to walk victoriously through the spiritual struggle and warfare that characterize human life.

Life as Strife

Jesus left no doubt, *"In the world you have tribulation* (trouble, anguish, distress), *but take courage; I have overcome the world"* (John 16:33). The reason this world is now organically oriented in a contrary way is found back in the Garden of Eden. Adam and Eve's disobedience to God brought a curse on the very soil of the earth that had once cooperated with and supported them (Genesis 3:17–19). Our habitat, at its most fundamental level, had become something resistant.

God also cursed Satan for deceiving Adam and Eve, declaring to him: *"I will put enmity* (hostility, animosity, antagonism) *between you and the woman, and between your seed and her seed"* (Genesis 3:15). At that moment strife became the way of life for all of us. Additionally, and most importantly for us, God has revealed that a more intense form of hatred is reserved for one particular group. *"So the dragon* [Satan] *was enraged with the woman, and went off to make war with the rest of her children, who keep the commandments of God and hold to the testimony of Jesus"* (Revelation 12:17 NIV). Obedient, faithful followers of Jesus are the focus of Satan's most intense animosity and activity.

This doesn't sound good, but take heart. We are not doomed to merely endure. We are destined to rise above and to reign. God intends us to see the fruit of our right walk, not only liberty and victory in our lives but the same for multiplying numbers of others along our path.

Our Guidebook

In giving us the Bible, God has given us everything we need for fully mature faith and for broad spectrum, real-life living. His Word is true and thus utterly trustworthy. As you enter this specific endeavor of learning and being empowered to follow Jesus faithfully through the spiritual dangers and struggles of life, the Bible will be your dependable guidebook and the little Book of Ephesians your primary source.

Ephesians is short but it is not shallow. It was written to the congregation in the great Asian city of Ephesus, probably in A.D. 62, by the apostle Paul while he was a prisoner in Rome. Paul had founded the church in Ephesus, laboring there for two years. First Church Ephesus was strong, solid, and influential. It had become the springhead of streams of living water flowing out all across the province of Asia. Now having been gone from them for nearly five years, Paul was greatly encouraged by reports of their faith and faithfulness. Despite planting the church there with many tears and trials, Paul did not shrink back from declaring to them *the whole purpose of God* and *anything that was profitable* (Acts 20:27, 20). On this comprehensive foundation as well as the testimony of their having lived out the full purposes of God, Paul now writes a letter, the height and breadth and practical depth of which are unparalleled.

Profession and Practice

Paul understood that what we *profess* to believe is not really what we believe. What we really believe is what our *lives* say we believe. Thus his letter to the Ephesians, in soaring fashion, presents clearly Jesus's relentless work to repair every place in our lives where practice is not connected to and directed by profession. Knowing and believing the truth is not enough. Where our behavior is not consistent with our beliefs, there we are still incapable of living out the full purposes for which we were born and reborn and there we are giving the enemy opportunity.

In the first half of Ephesians, Paul ranges across the full sweep of God's redemptive work, culminating in the pinnacle: our now being sealed in Him by the promised Holy Spirit and seated with Him in the heavenlies. Everything—EVERYTHING—has been placed under Jesus's feet, plus everyone—EVERYONE. There is no thing and no person and no authority, regardless of how wealthy or powerful, that is not under the dominion of Jesus. He is over all! And we are there with Him. What's more, He is over everything for a reason—us, His church. The church is the collective body of believers from all over the world in all of its varied local expressions. The church is Jesus's body here on earth, where He is working to live out His purpose of drawing all people to Himself.

Because He is the One who came after us when we were going the wrong way,
and because He is the One who paid our sin debt,
and because He is the One who actually saved us from ourselves,
and because we were handcrafted by Him for work He'd already planned for us,
We Must Walk Out That Work.

Not only does He have the plan, He has the power to perform it. He just calls us to come follow Him each day in wholehearted surrender and dependence. He will do the rest.

The Catch

Our passage through this world is intentionally not in a comfortable, climate-controlled car that insulates us from the world and its people. Instead, Jesus intends for our journey to be a walk. That way we don't hurry and we don't miss the opportunities all along the path. The catch is the world through which we walk and in which we do this work is enemy occupied. Thus, the walk isn't an easy stroll along cobblestone paths meandering through manicured gardens. Instead, the way generally is difficult and sometimes even dangerous. While it may seem that there are many contrary people along the path fighting against our works of love and witness, actually those working against us are spiritual beings who won't give up an inch or a life without a fight. Jesus knows that. He's made provision. He will work a transformation in you as you now walk through this *Strong Walk* experience with Him.

A Prerequisite

As I write these words, our youngest son is home from college for the summer. He has a full-time job and is saving his earnings toward next year's tuition. What he would really like to do this summer is work in the daytime and then "do stuff" in the evenings with his friends. Instead, each day, with his boss's permission, he leaves his job (and loses pay) to attend a class at the local community college. In the evenings, instead of fun "stuff," he has hard homework. Why is he doing this? Certainly not because it's pleasurable or even because he wants to. He is doing it because of something called a prerequisite. In order to continue his orderly and balanced development into a professional, he must first have the knowledge and skills that this particular summer course provides.

There is a direct parallel for you. In the culminating word (Ephesians 6:18) of what will be the focal passage of our transformational study, Paul strongly exhorts the believers: *"With all prayer and petition pray at all times in the Spirit, and with this in view, be on the alert with all perseverance and petition for all the saints."*

The primary means that God intends for us to employ in order to wage successful spiritual warfare is prayer; petitionary prayer, which is for ourselves, and intercessory prayer, which is for others. He isn't encouraging us to just increase our prayertime. God's intent is that life be prayertime. He wants us to walk out a life that is a prayer. In its fullest expression today, this is called being a lifestyle prayerwalker. My previous book *Follow Me* is a transformational tool in the hands of the only One who can teach us to pray and who can transform us into lifestyle pray-ers. Many thousands of believers have already walked through this study with other praying friends and know the joy and power of a life walked out in union with the Holy Spirit and a prayer life informed and empowered by the Holy Spirit.

If you have not already walked through *Follow Me*, just as Paul strongly exhorted the Ephesians to make "*all prayer . . . at all times*" their way of life, I urge you to pause at this point, lay *Strong Walk* aside for a few weeks, and walk through the *Follow Me* experience first. Just like our son's summer course, it may not be what you want to do; but since prayer is God's primary provision for waging and winning spiritual warfare, you will be very grateful that you did.

Finally

Now—either a few moments later or a few weeks later—you are probably saying, "Can I finally get to the reason I picked up *this* book in the first place?" You may not realize it when you say that, but that is exactly what Paul said, "*Finally*" (Ephesians 6:10). After laying out the full panorama of God's glorious work and its practical applications in everyday life, he now could finally say "*Finally*" and get to that which makes all the other possible; how to walk and war victoriously.

So, finally, let's get going.

About the Book

This may be the strangest request you've ever seen in a book but here goes:

Please don't read this book.

Yes, that's right. This book is not designed to teach you *about* spiritual warfare. Its sole intent is to see you transformed into a biblically shaped, spiritually empowered warrior. It is not about information. It is about transformation. If you read the book, you will be exposed to a lot of good information; but when you finish, there will be little, if any, change. Jesus is about change. Truth is for transformation. This book is a tool for our Lord to use, truth by truth, step by step, day by day, to change us. Resist the temptation to speed-read through this book. Instead, determine to follow Jesus through this pilgrimage, taking each step with Him, and allowing Him to bring steady, real change in who you are and how you live.

The structure is simple and the daily activities brief. It will take 30 minutes or less each morning to read and work through the material. If a morning quiet time has been a struggle for you, this book will help you strengthen that discipline in your life.

You certainly can go through the experience alone. But, as we will see later in the study, every single one of Paul's admonitions are in the second person plural. In some parts of our country, that would be translated "y'all." We are in this together. The Lord of the church intends for us to go through life together, and it is best if you go through this study the same way. Do you already have a group for whom this experience would be a natural fit? Your Bible study class? A missions group? A care group? A prayer team? Some friends that you socialize with? The experience will be enriched and there will be a higher level of mutual benefit and protection if you can go through it with others. You don't need a teacher. Jesus is the One who can, and will, teach us to pray and obey in the daily struggles of life. All you need is someone to facilitate the group's meetings and discussions. A facilitator's guide is provided for this purpose (it begins on p. 133).

Each day's experience contains six components—all brief, all vital.

- Our Weapon—His Word—a focused Scripture to speak into and over each day.
- Beginnings—a help to focus our minds on the Lord in praise and prayer.
- Our Study—open your Bible and let God transform with His truth.
- Through the Day—helps to build the truths of that day into our very being.
- Evening Reflections—Reflection means to think back on. I know that we rarely do this but we should. You will benefit from a few minutes of thinking back over your day—what God taught you, what you encountered, and how you responded.
- Our Way—Prayer—strategic prayer for ourselves and others.

Paul, in addressing a practical everyday issue, stated to Timothy, *"Give the enemy no opportunity"* (1 Timothy 5:14 NIV). As you walk through *Strong Walk,* God will be working to achieve this very same purpose in your life. So let it be.

First Week

Our Reigning King, Jesus

KEY SCRIPTURE

"Finally, be strong in the Lord and in the strength of His might" (Ephesians 6:10).

<u>*This week we will learn that Jesus is:*</u>

- Victorious
- Reigning
- Almighty
- Indwelling
- Guiding, providing
  and the significance these attributes have for me in spiritual warfare.

Week 1: Day 1
Jesus Is Victorious

Our Weapon—His Word

(Read aloud.)

"For He [God] rescued us from the domain of darkness, and transferred us to the kingdom of His beloved Son" (Colossians 1:13).

Beginnings

How glorious, on this first day, to celebrate the marvelous truth that we have been delivered from the kingdom of darkness and made citizens of Christ's wonderful kingdom of light and love. Bow and confess this reality, giving thanks to Him.

The Iraq war has reminded us of the connection between good intelligence and success on the battlefield. The more soldiers know about their enemy—his tendencies, his capabilities, his plans—the better able they are to defend themselves and conduct successful offensive operations. This is equally true for us—with a twist. Knowledge of our enemy is important, but more important for us as soldiers in this spiritual battle is knowledge of our Commander in Chief. To know Him is to know power in struggle, peace in war, and the promise of victory in our own lives.

Open your Bible to 1 John 3:8. Why did Jesus come to earth?

Yes, He came to destroy the works of the devil. And the works of our enemy are always counter to the purposes of God.

What is God's ultimate purpose? (2 Peter 3:9) _____

And what is Satan's? (John 10:10*a*) _____

God's great desire is that people not perish in their sin but instead, as sheep, come to hear and listen to the voice of the Great Shepherd, and allow Him to lead them to safety and provision. Satan, by contrast, doesn't want life for people. He wants death, and he always works to that end.

Supremely, this was his goal from the beginning regarding Jesus. From an oblique reference, it may actually have been that when he became aware that the Savior was going to be born, he waited before the woman, like the ravenous lion that he is, *"that . . . he might devour her child"* (Revelation 12:4). In King Herod he found a powerful ally who, at the time of the birth of *the* King, ordered all the baby boys killed, believing that this would ensure the death of the one baby who might supplant him (Matthew 2:16–23). That plot, too, was unsuccessful. So, biding his time, Satan waited for years until Jesus was led into the wilderness. There he launched a three-stage temptation (Matthew 4:1–11). This attempt fared no better than the others. Finally, putting into the heart of Judas to betray Jesus into the hands of the Jewish and Roman leaders, he gained his ultimate desire (Luke 22:1–6). The one threat to his terminal control over people was finally eliminated. At last. Success.

God's great desire is that people not perish in their sin.

Look to Ephesians 1:19–20. Did Satan's plan really succeed?____

_____

No. Actually, God succeeded in His plan. He raised Jesus back to life and He is now the Victor—over Satan and over death and over the great separator—sin. He lives and now we can live too.

Through the Day

Pause at moments through today and think on this truth: Satan did not win. Jesus did. And because that is the truth, I can be a winner as well.

Evening Reflections

As you consciously made the effort to consider this supreme truth, what other thoughts or feelings did you have?

Did the enemy try to plant doubt in your mind?

How did you respond?

Our Way—Prayer

"Father, thank You that no matter how hard or distressing life has been up to now, it can change because Jesus is the Victor and He is mine and I am His. Hallelujah."

Week 1: Day 2

Jesus Is Reigning

Our Weapon—His Word

(Read aloud.)

"He raised Him from the dead, and seated Him at his right hand in the heavenly places, far above all rule and authority and power and dominion, and every name that is named, not only in this age but also in the one to come. And He put all things in subjection under His feet, and gave Him as head over all things" (Ephesians 1:20–22).

Beginnings

Jesus not only was victorious in the most critical battle of earthly history, He has now been given the place of supreme honor and supreme power over not only earth, but all the universe. Jesus calls *all* the shots. He reigns! At the start of this day, celebrate our reigning King—Jesus.

It's been said, "Perception is reality." How we perceive things does determine not just how life looks to us but how life actually *is* for us. But over and above this truism is the suprareality (that is, the way things really are). The enemy would have us believe that the two, perception and reality, are really just one. The way things seem is the way they are. No chance of change.

This morning, let's begin by opening our Bibles to John 16:33. What does Jesus say life in this world is going to be characterized by?

Yes, tribulation, or difficult trials. This is what life here *is* like. So based on this truth, our perception then of all of life is likely what?

_____

Yes, trouble.

Now let's look again at Jesus's Word and read on to the end of the verse. What is the suprareality over this perception? _____

_____

That's right. Jesus has overcome the distressing pattern of continually troubled life in this world. Thus we can and must *"take courage."*

Why are we encouraged? Because He is far above it all? Probably not, because while He's in heaven, we're still here. Or are we?

Turn now to Ephesians 2:4–6 and read.

Are we really still stuck in this depressing mess? We're not, are we? When we turned back to Him, God not only made us alive, He moved us. Our walk is still with Him on this earth, but positionally we are now seated with Him in heaven. Perspective makes all the difference in perception. Looking up, we long for something better. Looking down, we live the something better.

Which brings us to another paradox of the Christian life. Our walking has, as its foundational activity, sitting. Seems impossible but it's true. And while true, it is difficult to understand and even more difficult to live out.

The story is told (whether true, I have been unable to verify) of the tightrope walker who had a cable stretched across Niagara Falls. On the appointed day, to the anxious adulation of the crowd, he proceeded not only to walk across the falls but then push a wheelbarrow across. Quieting the cheering crowd, he asked if they believed that he could now push the wheelbarrow back across with a person in it. With great fervor, the crowd shouted, "Yes!" But when he asked for someone to come up and get in the wheelbarrow, no one moved.

Jesus reigns over all.

To go with Jesus through this dangerous world, we will not only have to trust Him to get us to the other side, we will have to sit down and let Him. Simultaneous sitting and walking seem to be mutually exclusive, but they are not. Positionally we sit. Practically we walk. Our rest is in Him. Our obedience is in walking with Him.

Through the Day

Think on this. Jesus reigns over all. Much of daily life seems to indicate that someone else does. But that's not true. Jesus does. Invite Him to reign in you today. And consciously stay in the position God has placed you: seated with Him in the throne room of the universe.

Evening Reflections

How did it go as you intentionally rested in Him today while you went about your work?

At what points did you feel you couldn't trust Him?

Ask His forgiveness for those instances and place yourself solidly back in His care.

Our Way—Prayer

"Lord, I thank You that You reign over all the earth and all there is. Reign in me. Help me sit and rest in You. And tomorrow give me the power to follow You in that trust. Amen."

Our Weapon—His Word

(Read aloud.)

Jesus said, "All authority has been given to Me in heaven and on earth. Go therefore and make disciples of all the nations" (Matthew 28:18–19).

Beginnings

How glorious to start the day with the fresh realization that my place is seated with Him. Today I can rest in Him and let Him meet the needs of the day as I follow Him through it. Give Him thanks saying, "Lead on, O King Eternal."

Let's turn to Colossians 1:16. We know that everything in heaven and on earth, both the visible and the invisible, is now under the authority of Jesus, our Lord.

Who created all of this? _____

And for whom was it all created? _____

The answer to both questions is Jesus. It was created by Him and for Him, for His use and ultimately for His glory.

Now turn back to Ephesians 6:12. While it seems that our struggle is with difficult, even mean people, who actually is our struggle with?

_____

Yes, the very powers and authorities that Jesus Himself created for His purposes. Right now they are, superficially, under the direction of Satan; but ultimately they are under the sovereign control of the Ruler of the universe, Jesus, our Lord. And so is Satan himself. We will study this in more depth in a couple of weeks; but for now it is sufficient to state, regardless of how life may look or seem at times, Jesus is in control. Satan is not. There are people and places where the enemy has varying degrees of influence, but he is already defeated and under the authority of Jesus who is always working *"all things after the counsel of His will"* (Ephesians 1:11).

Look now at the end of chapter 1, verses 22–23. For whom was everything put under the authority of Jesus? _____

That's right. For us, the church. It may seem that the church is often insignificant in the flow of earthly events, that it is on the sidelines. It is not. The church is at the center of it all and the world, regardless of perception, is on the periphery. Jesus rules it all and supremely, at the center, He rules the church. The church is us, the body that He indwells and through which He lives out His love. The church is how He fills all the earth with His presence and His glory.

Why then are many people and many parts of the earth not yet acknowledging His presence, enjoying His glory, and giving Him praise? Much of His body, the church, is not walking with Him in obedience and abandon.

So He says, "Follow Me out into the world today and fill your place in it by resting in Me. I have been working all the details and circumstances of your day today to advance My purposes. Extend My glory and presence in the world by showing My love to someone that I bring near you. Tell them of My love for them. They, too, need to come back home."

> *Jesus is in control. Satan is not.*

Through the Day

Today the unlimited power of Jesus is ours in whatever He has arranged for us to face. Stay at rest in His strength and stay ready to respond to His plan. Be sure to think about this truth: Jesus has all power and authority.

Evening Reflections

What opportunity did Jesus provide you today to extend His kingdom?

How did you meet that opportunity?

How did you experience His power to live?

Our Way—Prayer

"Lord, how matchless is Your power and sovereignty. I praise You this evening and thank You for the peace that Your rule gives me. May I rest in Your care this night. Amen."

Week 1: Day 4

Jesus Is Indwelling

Our Weapon—His Word

(Read aloud.)

"Behold, I stand at the door and knock; if anyone hears My voice and opens the door, I will come in to him and will dine with him, and he with Me" (Revelation 3:20).

Beginnings

When John encountered the One who said these words, he fell on the ground as if dead (Revelation 1:17). May we be sobered this morning at the realization that this same Jesus comes from highest heaven and stands at the door of our lives, seeking entrance. Invite Him in to reign in your life today. Enjoy His sweet presence. Let Him have His way in you.

The world offers us a near endless list of ways to live. The truth is, though, we can't live. And the reason? We are already dead in our trespasses and sins (Ephesians 2:1) and everyone knows that the dead don't have the power in themselves to live again. But God, because of His rich mercy and love, does have that power and He made us truly alive in Jesus (Ephesians 2:4–5).

And when we are made alive by responding to His knock, inviting Him into our lives as Lord, He comes in the person of His Spirit, the One known as the Holy Spirit.

When Nicodemus came to Jesus, inquiring about these puzzling things that Jesus was teaching, Jesus went right to the heart of the issue of living when we're already dead. Look at John 3:5. What does Jesus say?

Yes, of course, a person has to be born in the normal, natural way; but the natural life, even lived in devotion and service to God, cannot earn merit sufficient to be acceptable to God. That life must be born again, by the Holy Spirit, for new life to come. At that point we become adopted children of the King. We are in the family. We are in Him (Galatians 4:4–6).

Invite Him in to reign in your life today. Enjoy His sweet presence.

Now look to 2 Corinthians 5:17. What happens when we are "in Christ"? _____

_____

Yes, gloriously, everything becomes new. Now we can live. And it is Jesus, living in us by His Spirit that makes this possible.

Turn now to Romans 8:6–16. The passage is a bit long but worth our attention because here Paul clearly states how this "new life" reality is possible while we still live in the "old life" body. The answer: the Spirit. He gives life to our bodies and enables and empowers us to live to Him and not to ourselves.

So when the enemy comes at you, tempting you to turn back to the ways of the flesh and the world, remember:

- You are in Christ. That's who you are and where you are.
- Satan is coming at you because he wants to keep you from being all God wants you to be.
- He is really coming at Jesus because you are in Him and he can't get to you except through Him.
- He is coming at the same Jesus who has already defeated him.
- He is coming at the same Jesus who has ultimate authority over him.

So stay at rest in Jesus, trusting Him and following Him. And when pain or suffering comes (and it will) remember,

"The sufferings of this present time are not worthy to be compared with the glory that is to be revealed to us" (Romans 8:18).

Through the Day

As you move through today, acknowledge Jesus's ruling presence in you by His Spirit. Be alert to what the Spirit may warn you about, may prompt you to say, and then do as He directs. He indwells to give you every good thing necessary for real life.

Evening Reflections

How did the Holy Spirit speak to you today?

Did you respond?

What was life in Him like today?

Our Way—Prayer

"Savior, how precious is life in You. Thank You for giving me this life and for living in me that I might have Your power to live it. I rest in You tonight."

Week 1: Day 5
Jesus Guides and Provides

Our Weapon—His Word

(Read aloud.)

"I am the vine, you are the branches; he who abides in Me and I in him, he bears much fruit, for apart from Me you can do nothing" *(John 15:5).*

Beginnings

Today, as every day, Jesus wants us to remember that we do not produce the fruit. We are His body through which He lives today. We are the vehicle through which He produces fruit today. So intentionally stay at rest in Him, abiding not striving. That way He can do what He purposes through you today.

In the midst of perhaps the most intimate time for Jesus with His disciples (in the upper room just before His betrayal), Jesus inserts a common yet powerful symbol into the flow of words. Set in the majesty and import of what He is saying to the disciples (John 14 and 15), the metaphor, at first, seems both simplistic and inappropriate. In fact, it is profound.

A metaphor is a word that, while not directly related to a topic, carries a resemblance that enhances understanding of the real topic. Open your Bible to John 15 and read the first five verses. What is the metaphor Jesus uses here? _____

In choosing the grapevine, Jesus, in an instant, mentally transports the disciples to a vineyard and central to the setting there would be clusters of grapes, the symbol to the Jews that forever reminds them of the bounty of Jehovah toward them.

Who does the vine represent? _____

Who does the branch represent?_____

And who is the vinedresser? _____

When we became daughters and sons of God, He did this by grafting us into the one True Vine, Jesus. We are not daughters and sons by birth. We are adopted. Before turning and returning, we were wild things and we lived like it. He is the One who sought us. He's the One who bought us. He wooed and He waited. And when finally we took that first step back, we were grafted into Him, the one True Vine. At that moment the old life was left behind. Now we have a new life and it is as an extension of His life. We are branches.

In this relationship, He guides by determining which direction we grow, who we touch, how we express His inner beauty, the kind of fruit we bear, and on and on. He does all of this as the Vine.

He also provides and we do one thing. We make sure nothing hinders the flow of His life into ours. And what hinders His life in us? *Sin.* Often this sin is expressed through resistance and self-will. Isn't it ludicrous to think that a branch would resist the vine? Branches inherently know that they have no life in and of themselves. Their life is found in the Vine and flows from it to them. That's why Jesus could say, *"Apart from Me you can do nothing."*

Guidance and provision, the vine and branch—but there is one more aspect to the vineyard metaphor. What was that? _____

Yes, the Vinedresser who is God, our Father. He prunes the branches, cutting away what shouldn't be allowed to remain, not so the branch's life is less (although during and right after pruning it may appear that way), but that the branch's life may be more. In Hebrews 12:4–11 this pruning is called discipline. Two points here are critical for us as spiritual warriors.

- Don't resist the Vine or the Vinedresser. They have a plan and they know what they are doing. Trust them.

- Don't confuse the pain of discipline with spiritual warfare. Discipline is not from the devil. It is from God for good. Cooperate.

Through the Day

Make sure today, that Jesus, the Vine, can do *whatever* He wants through your life. Declare it and then watch for how He does it.

Evening Reflections

Did you resist allowing Jesus free rein in your life today?
How?

Confess it and turn loose of it.

What about any fears?

He is worthy of your trust. As you lie down to sleep, trust in His care. His perfect love casts out fear.

Our Way—Prayer

"Master, thank You for the fresh realization that my life is Your life and that the picture of a connected branch really is simple and helpful. Help me let You make connection a growing reality in my life. Amen."

Second Week

Our

Equipment

"Put on the full armor of God, so that you will be able to stand firm against the schemes of the devil" (Ephesians 6:11).

This week we will learn the equipment that Jesus has provided and how to use it:

- Truth
- Righteousness
- The gospel of peace
- Faith and salvation
- The Word and prayer

Week 2: Day 1
Truth Is Central

Our Weapon—His Word

(Read aloud.)
"Put on . . . that you will be able to stand firm" (Ephesians 6:11).

Beginnings

Last year, as our son approached an intersection, a driver made a left turn in front of him and was violently reminded that you shouldn't do that. There are several parallels between the accident and what we are about to learn during this critically important week of transformational study.

- While the driver making the turn was alert and busy about his day's business, he had no idea that a serious collision was just ahead.
- The driver wasn't physically injured, but he was definitely shaken up and his ability to continue functioning normally was hindered.
- Someone was responsible for what happened.
- Having been a defensive driving instructor years ago, I can say, categorically, defensive driving would have prevented the crash.

Praise God this morning that He knows what lies ahead today and that He is not only watching out for us, He is also teaching us how to walk and war defensively.

This week we will study the defensive parts of the armor that God has given us and how to use them to "stand firm" (protect ourselves) against the enemy's plans. Our success as spiritual warriors depends on knowing how to use this armor, so let's pause, bow before the Lord, and ask Him to open up our understanding. Now, as we move forward along the path of His answering your prayer, we can be assured that He will accomplish that in us.

Parallel Point 1. Critical to victorious spiritual warfare is the realization that at any moment a collision could be dead ahead. Because of this, we are warned to be vigilant, always on the alert (1 Peter 5:8*a*). In the spiritual realm, these potential collisions are power collisions, the power of the enemy and his forces colliding with the power of Christ in His followers. One moment we may be going about Christ's business and the next moment, wrecked by an oncoming vehicle that we didn't see.

Parallel Point 2. The force of these collisions may not physically injure us (although the potential is always there), but it does shake us up spiritually and emotionally and thus can impair our ability to function again at the same or a higher level.

Parallel Point 3. We are responsible. God gives what we need, but it's up to us to use it. Read Ephesians 6:14–15. While it is not plain in the English translation, the form of the Greek verbs that Paul uses here to present these first pieces of the armor carries the requirement that *we* put them on. If we don't, either out of ignorance or out of negligence, we are what is called "an accident looking for a place to happen." And be assured, our scheming enemy has an intersection already picked out.

Parallel Point 4. Just like a defensive driving course, Jesus has a defensive walking course in which He will teach us everything we need to know to walk with Him through this dangerous world. Would you like to guess where you can find that course? You're right, in the Bible and, most comprehensively, in the Book of Ephesians.

Using the analogy of a warrior's armor, Paul in Ephesians 6 gives us the first component of this defensive walking course—truth (v. 14). *"Having girded your loins with truth."* The battle always begins with truth. Later we will study in more detail the first effort of the enemy to attack us (the Garden of Eden) and we will find that it was a truth encounter. In wily power, he came against Adam and Eve. Because they were unclear about what God

> *God gives what we need. It's up to us to use it.*

had said, their wreck was so severe it wrecked the world and the whole human race. We call that wreck the Fall.

So, be on guard and know the truth because Satan will attack you at this very same point.

The Holy Spirit guided Paul to relate truth to the belt, which was always the first piece of the armor put on. As the belt encircled the loins (the waist—the place the Jews believed was the center of a person's strength and power), so we must ensure that our lives are encircled by God's truth. We make sure we live surrounded by His truth because the world around us is full of lies masquerading as truth. Formerly, we lived lives that were a lie. Now, though, we know personally the truth of Jesus's words, *"You will know the truth, and the truth will make you free"* (John 8:32).

The pinnacle of God's truth is the gospel, the good news of salvation, and this good news is "the power of God" (Romans 1:16) that makes us alive. When the power collisions of earthly life come, we are victorious because it is Satan's power running into God's power. Our enemy is always the loser in that encounter.

Through the Day

Thank God that truth is a safe circle in which we can live. Repeatedly today, remember the good news (the gospel) was God's power to set you free and is God's power to keep you free. Doing that, you are immediately more able to live in line with His truth.

Evening Reflections

Did you recognize a point today when your life was out of line with what you knew to be the truth?

Did you then immediately line back up with what you knew was right and true?

Our Way—Prayer

"Loving Master, thank You that you created us to live in relationship and thank You that You made it possible for us to again live in relationship with You and others. Your truth makes that possible. I want it to be ever more so. Help me."

Our Weapon—His Word

(Read aloud.)

"Stand firm therefore, having girded your loins with truth, and having put on the breastplate of righteousness" (Ephesians 6:14).

Beginnings

What a thought! The truth of the gospel *is* the power of God to set me free and keep me free. All thanks and praise to Jesus, our Savior. Invite Him to teach you today how to use truth and righteousness to stand more firmly against the devil.

Often we think the latest way is the best way. The newest program, the latest technique fascinate us because, frankly, we've been conditioned to accept new as better than old.

As followers of Jesus, though, the old way, the biblical way, is always the best way. In recent years we have seen many new spiritual warfare techniques and strategies introduced. Some are biblical. Many are not. What makes something biblical? In a word: consistency with biblical truth. Rather than enhancing biblically consistent living, new techniques often end up supplanting it.

Read James 4:7. What are we instructed to do regarding God?

_____

Regarding Satan? _____

Now read 1 Peter 5:9. Again, what are we instructed to do concerning God? _____ Concerning Satan?

_____

In Ephesians and other passages God instructs us to remain firm in our faith, submitting to Him while we resist the evil one. The New Testament church modeled this. Always at the heart of its advance against the spiritual forces of darkness we find faithful resistance.

Look again at Ephesians 6:14. How does God intend truth, belted around us, to be the first step in our successful resistance? In the introduction I mentioned to you that what we profess to believe is not really what we believe. Do you remember what I said reveals our true beliefs? Yes. It's what our life says we believe, and that is what Paul is indicating to us here. When he instructs us to belt on or put on truth, he is telling us to consciously live under the influence of the truth, especially the mighty power of the good news. We do this simply, intentionally, by remembering and confessing that the good news, the gospel, *was* the power to set us free and *is* the power to keep us free. (Do that right now before going any further.)

When we do this, we take off the old way of thinking which was inconsistent with God's truth and consciously begin to live out His truth. A technical way to say this is subjective truth (what we think of and orient to as truth) will be lined up with objective truth (God's truth, real truth).

My wife is a certified public accountant. Sometimes when she answers people's questions according to the requirements of the law, they don't like it. Why? The truth doesn't fit what they want to do. At that point they face a decision. Will they do what is right or will they do what they wish were right?

As you read in God's Word each day, study it, think about it, declare it (as we do at the start of each day of this study), you are equipping yourself to "let the word of Christ richly dwell within you" (Colossians 3:16). You are encircling your life with His truth. His truth has His power and that is why His truth transforms.

A beautiful and practical complement to this is that truth shows the lie of the world. Remember that recognition is the first step to rejection. Truth enables us to recognize lies, especially the cleverly disguised ones, so we can reject them and live truly. Make sure you do.

When we do what is right, we strip the enemy of opportunity.

And now what about righteousness (that is, goodness, purity, uprightness)? How can we put on righteousness when, although we were created that way originally (Ecclesiastes 7:29), we don't have it anymore? It was lost in the Fall. We can't put on a bulletproof vest of righteousness if we don't have one. Since the breastplate protects the heart, so critical to life, does anyone know where we might get this critical piece of protection? Could we possibly work and earn enough to buy it?

Turn to Philippians 3:8–9. Who has righteousness? _____
_____

How can we get it? _____

When we place our faith in Christ, He gives us His righteousness. How amazing! Now when God looks at us, He sees us as pure and good, because when He looks at us, He sees Christ's goodness. Remember this. His pure goodness is our bulletproof vest (breastplate) and we keep it on, protecting our heart, by confessing this truth with our lips and by confessing this truth with our lives (by refusing to carry on with the old works of our old lives such as jealousy, lying, lusting, stealing, etc.). In giving us His goodness, Christ has totally defeated the enemy. In turn Christ's goodness transforms our lives into good and pure living.

When we do what is right, we strip the enemy of opportunity. When we don't, we put the welcome mat out for him.

Through the Day

Think on these realities: I can never work hard enough or be good enough to be accepted by God. But, praise Him, I already am because my Savior saved me and gave me His goodness. Oh, what power is now mine to live truly and act rightly.

Declare this as you go through the day and ask the Spirit of Truth to show you any place where your believing and living are not consistent with truth and rightness.

Evening Reflections

Did the Spirit reveal any inconsistency in your living today?

Did you immediately turn away from it and ask His forgiveness?

Our Way—Prayer

"Savior, how wonderful is life lived truly and rightly. Thank You that You are the One who makes that possible for me. Bury truth and right deeply within me as I sleep. I love You. I thank You."

Week 2: Day 3
Gospel Peace Readies Us for Victory

Our Weapon—His Word

(Read aloud.)

"And having shod your feet with the preparation of the gospel of peace" *(Ephesians 6:15).*

Beginnings

Give Him thanks for the good rest of last night and the deepened reality of His truth and goodness in you. Already He is increasing your strength to stand firm against the plots of the enemy. As you thank God in prayer, ask Him to continue giving understanding as today we add the gospel of peace to our armor.

Do you have a gate at your residence? _____
What is its purpose? _____
A gate is a moveable blockade used to control access to a yard or a field or, in earlier times, to a city. Now look at Matthew 16:18. What does Jesus say concerning His church? _____

The gates of hell shall not be able to hold out against His church as it follows Him in advance upon the places where Satan holds captive precious people. Jesus came to proclaim release to the captives (Luke 4:18) and they will be set free.

As we add another piece of the armor today, let us be sure to grasp an important truth. While each piece of the armor is given to us for defensive purposes, to protect us, the church of Jesus is not on the defensive. We are on the offensive and our armor is to provide protection for us as we advance.

Look at Ephesians 6:15. Notice first what this piece of the armor is *not.* Despite a common assumption, it is not the gospel. Instead, what is it? _____

Yes, that's right. It is the readiness, the preparation, that the gospel of peace brings. When the gospel brings peace, we are ready for warfare. The shoes or sandals were to protect the feet of the soldier and enable him to be sure-footed and quick. The good news of freedom found in Christ unburdens us from the sin we formerly carried. Also, the weight of the enemy's accusations and condemnations has been off-loaded. Lastly, the awful burden that our self-willed life brought is gone. We are at peace with God. And—this is beautiful—no longer being at odds with God makes us ready, even eager, to do battle with the enemy who had so much to do with the painful life we once lived. The liberating gospel both prepares us and gives us courage to march into enemy-held areas and see others set free.

Always keep this next point in mind. An exhaustive study of the Book of Acts reveals that while the church did occasionally have direct confrontations with demonic forces, primarily the spiritual warfare of the early church had four components: praying, living, standing, and proclaiming. Overwhelmingly, the predominant activity was proclaiming the good news of the gospel. As we follow the New Testament model in our warfare, we must be diligent to abundantly sow the seed of the gospel, that God might bring the great harvest that He so desires.

> *Because of your faith in Jesus, salvation has come. You are at peace with God.*

Research indicates that it now takes 86 church members to see one person publicly confess Christ through baptism. If we go out into the world generously spreading the seed of the gospel, we will, without a doubt, come back with an abundant harvest (Psalm 126:6; Isaiah 55:10–11). We have to conclude: we are not sowing abundantly.

Remember, the gospel *"is the power of God for salvation to everyone who believes"* (Romans 1:16). Every day the enemy will flee from us as we live it and share it.

Through the Day

As you move into today's activities, consider the marvelous reality that because of your faith in Jesus, salvation has come. You are at peace with God. That alone makes you ready to stand against the enemy's efforts to draw you back into the old life. Resist him, strong in your faith.

Evening Reflections

Did God give you opportunity to testify today of your life in Christ?

How did that feel?

How did the person respond?

Our Way—Prayer

"Master, I thank You with all my heart for the realization that Your salvation prepares me to stand confident against the enemy. And I thank You that Your gospel is Your power in me to resist the devil."

Week 2: Day 4

Faith and Salvation

Our Weapon—His Word

(Read aloud.)

"In addition to all, taking up the shield of faith with which you will be able to extinguish all the flaming arrows of the evil one. And take the helmet of salvation" (Ephesians 6:16–17).

Beginnings

Isn't the growing gratitude in our hearts wonderful as we progressively realize that in the gospel God has provided everything we need for life and victory? Thank Him and then ask Him to show you today any point where your life is not lining up with Christ's life, thus making you vulnerable to the devil's designs.

Perhaps in a beachfront gift shop you have seen beautiful seashells for sale. My favorite is a certain family of mollusks. On the outside they are rough and ugly, but after turning them over my eye is captured by the exquisite iridescence of a substance called mother-of-pearl. Looking at words, particularly in Bible study, can be like looking at mollusk shells. On the outside nothing may seem that special, but what we find on the inside is of great beauty and value.

When we look inside Paul's instructive words in Ephesians 6:10–17 (*"be strong"; "put on"; "take up"; "stand firm"; "having girded"; "having put on"; "having shod";* etc.) two important aspects appear.

- These are imperative, forceful words. These are not suggestions. They are requirements. To walk as obedient followers of Jesus, these are things we have to do.

- Each word is in the second person plural. They are not addressed to us individually but to us as part of the body, the church. "All of you" put on, take up, stand firm, etc. We are in this together and we need each other.

These two truths have special significance as we look at the next piece of our armor, the shield. Look at verse 16. What does Paul say the shield represents? _____

Yes, faith. In the Old Testament the shield is often used as a metaphor for the protection of God. When we place our faith in Him, we step in behind His protection. As a warrior fought from behind his shield, so do we. As a warrior would not think of going into battle without his shield, so neither should we. The shield was not optional; neither is faith.

Everyone believes in or trusts in something. Only as our faith is anchored in God can we confidently expect to be successful in battling our enemy. The act of our faith is powerful because of the object of our faith—God. He is ever faithful and all-powerful.

We are in this struggle together and we need each other.

To truly understand the metaphor, we need to know how the shields were used. Roman shields were about four feet long and covered most of the body. In battle formation, as the soldiers advanced, their shields overlapped that of the soldier beside them. Thus each soldier not only protected himself but his fellow soldier. This picture is revealing for us as spiritual warriors. Our faith provides sure cover for us as well as those that God has placed with us. We are in this struggle together and we need each other.

Now, the helmet. For us as spiritual warriors what is it? (Ephesians 6:17) _____

It is indeed God's great salvation. A helmet covers the head, the center of thought and consideration. Whenever the enemy seeks to strike a blow of doubt or temptation, the helmet wards it off. Perhaps the ultimate blow is that of doubt regarding the love and acceptance of God. Our helmet, His great salvation, forever keeps Satan from striking that disastrous blow. We *are* loved (1 John 4:8–10). We *are* accepted (Romans 15:7). Keep the helmet on. His salvation guards our minds.

Through the Day

Whatever kind of flaming arrow may be directed at you today, don't let it rattle you or scare you into dropping your shield. Hold it firm. Believe in God. Remember your salvation. Keep that helmet on. Doubts and impure thoughts will not gain entrance.

Evening Reflections

Often when the enemy sees us growing in knowledge of the ways of God, he seeks to intensify his attacks. Did he do so against you today?

How did you respond?

Our Way—Prayer

"Mighty Savior, it is so wonderful to gain new ground of understanding in resisting the devil and seeing him flee from me. Thank You. All praise to You. I lie down in the reality of Your salvation and ask You to guard my mind as I rest tonight in Your care."

Week 2: Day 5
Prayer and the Word

Our Weapon—His Word

(Read aloud.)

"And take . . . the sword of the Spirit, which is the word of God. With all prayer and petition pray at all times in the Spirit, and with this in view, be on the alert with all perseverance and petition for all the saints" (Ephesians 6:17–18).

Beginnings

In our coat closet, I have two heavy coats, an older brown one and a newer blue one. Each winter morning I go to that closet and consider which one I will put on. I can get by with the old one (I have for a long time) but the newer one is better suited in every way for the cold weather and winter wind. It's the same for us as spiritual warriors. We can get by with what we have always put on. But why would we want to when God has given us an outfit, perfect in every way, for what we will face? Consciously, make the right choice—the full armor of God. Otherwise, unconsciously, you will reach for the old.

On this last day of our week, let's review the elements that Jesus has given us for protection.

First is truth. Just as you would think me foolish if you saw me putting on the newer coat over the old coat (and I would certainly look foolish), so are we foolish to think we can put on the new coat of truth over the old coat of living lies. Truth is always the pivot point in spiritual warfare. We have to know the truth (so continue to study and think on His Word) and then make the choice to believe it and not the lies of the world. That's how we belt on truth.

Second is righteousness. Even though in America there is a move to teach that we all are inherently good, we are not. We have all sinned. We all are far short of the purity and goodness of God. But since our Savior is wholly righteous, when we placed our faith in Him, He gave us His righteousness. Our hearts are now protected as if we each had on a bulletproof vest. His righteousness enables us to live righteously. We've put it on. Keep it on.

Third is the preparation the gospel gives. When I put on my newer winter coat, I'm ready for anything winter can throw at me. Why would I want to take it off? God has lifted the load of sin and guilt. Don't let the enemy tempt you back into any aspect of the old life. Keep walking in the peace that the gospel brought you. You're ready to follow Jesus into battle. Stay that way.

Fourth is faith. Regardless of what comes at you from the enemy in the form of accusation, temptation, condemnation, etc., keep believing in and trusting God. These things will fizzle right out. Whatever you do, trust Him.

And fifth is salvation. We're loved. We're accepted. We're saved. We're His. Don't doubt it and you will keep your mind protected.

Now we look at the last two elements of the full complement of our spiritual weaponry. One is the final piece of the armor, the sword, which is the Word of God. And the last, prayer, while not a piece of the armor is foundational to the successful use of it all.

Turn to Matthew 4:1–11. Here we find a graphic example of the use of the Word of God in warfare with the devil. What did Jesus do each time the enemy attacked Him with temptations? _____

> *Don't let the enemy tempt you back into any aspect of the old life.*

Yes, He responded with the Word of God.

Also, notice Ephesians 6:17. Who gives the Word its edge, its effectiveness? _____

It is the Holy Spirit indeed. Attacks by the enemy are repulsed as we first parry them and then counter them with the Word of God made sharp by the Spirit of God.

(Have you noticed that every morning I have been asking you to read aloud the focus Scripture? In this way you practice this very aspect of spiritual warfare. Declare the truth right up front. Put the sword out ahead, ready for the enemy's thrusts.)

And, lastly, prayer. We've already stressed the pervasive importance of living a life that is a prayer and the truth that continuous (*"at all times"*) prayer is the primary means that God intends for us to wage and win spiritual warfare.

Look at Ephesians 6:18. How does God intend for us to pray at all times? _____

Yes, in the Spirit (that is, in union with the Holy Spirit, guided and animated by Him and His knowledge of God's desires). We are to stay vigilant, persevering in prayer for all the body of Christ.

Living in union with Christ by prayer, each piece of our protective armor in place, and the Word of God in hand and ready, we *can* stand firm against the schemes of the devil!

And in living this way, we ensure that we *"give the enemy no opportunity"* as we march humbly and confidently forward into setting captives free with the gospel.

Through the Day

I know that you are shouting "Hallelujah!" (Well, at least you are whispering it.) Praise God. How wonderful and powerful are His provisions for us His children. Thank Him throughout this day.

Evening Reflections

Was the day a glorious one of praise and thanksgiving?

Did the enemy try to dim your joy?

Did you respond with the Word of God?

Our Way—Prayer

"Thank You, Lord, for how You have answered my prayer over these two weeks as I have sought to know You better and understand Your provisions for me in the spiritual struggles that characterize life. Guard me and guide me as I follow You forward."

Third Week

Our
Enemy

"Your adversary, the devil, prowls about like a roaring lion, seeking someone to devour" (1 Peter 5:8).

<u>*This week we will learn that our adversary is:*</u>

- Defeated
- Dangerous
- Scheming
- A liar
- In subjection

Week 3: Day 1
Our Defeated Enemy

Our Weapon—His Word

(Read aloud.)

"The dragon and his angels waged war, and they were not strong enough, and there was no longer a place found for them in heaven. And the great dragon was thrown down, the serpent of old who is called the devil and Satan" (Revelation 12:7–9).

Beginnings

Strengthened with fresh realizations of our mighty King and readied with His provisions for the battlefields ahead, we begin this week of necessary yet sobering study of our enemy with a glorious declaration. He has been thrown down. He is defeated. Hallelujah! All glory and honor to our great God.

A phone conversation with a longtime and trusted intercessory friend came around to a mutual observation: when it comes to the devil, we either give him too much attention or too little. As I reflected on that I remembered something that tells me that not a lot has changed. C. S. Lewis wrote, in his classic, *The Screwtape Letters*, of the same reality.

"There are two equal and opposite errors into which our race can fall about the devils. One is to disbelieve in their existence. The other is to believe, and to feel an excessive and unhealthy interest in them. They themselves are equally pleased by both."

Surveys show that the majority of Americans still believe in the devil; but for the most part our national error is giving too little, not too much, credence to his character and his purposes. Satan is present, active, and dangerous. But having said that, the more important thing to remember is this: He is defeated. Inherent in Christ's words on the Cross, "It is finished," is this fact: Satan is finished. We see this as we look at today's Scripture focus (Revelation 12:7ff.). Read verses 7–8 first. What was lost? _____

Yes, the one who once had unfettered access to God, continuously spewing out his vile accusations against God's servants (v. 10), lost his platform. Jesus is not only eternally victorious over sin and death but also over the devil.

As we consider a few questions about Satan and spiritual warfare, let's keep this foundational truth in mind: God, in His Word, has given us all we need to answer any question that we need answered regarding believing and living. With that reiterated, let's raise some frequently asked questions.

Is Satan a created being? Yes, definitely. Nowhere does Scripture indicate that he is preexistent or of the divine nature of the Trinity.

Can he simultaneously be in multiple places at the same time? No, he is finite. He can only be in one place at a time. However, his spiritual forces are vast beyond our knowing; and when those humans who are under his power are included, we see how he can influence multiple events through these others.

Is he a former high-ranking heavenly being who became filled with pride and self-will? Yes, it seems so; though it's not 100 percent clear (Isaiah 14:12–17; Ezekiel 28:12–19).

Did He lead a cosmic rebellion against God? Throughout Scripture a rebellion in heaven with Satan as the leader is treated as fact. The rebellion likely went on for an extended period of time.

Did Satan have a host of traitorous angels with him, possibly even a third of heaven's angels? Yes, and possibly yes (Revelation 12:7 and Revelation 12:4).

Are these "fallen" angels one and the same with *Satan is defeated.* the demons and evil spirits portrayed in the New Testament? Their character and evil activities are certainly similar.

As we consider these points, let's guard against majoring on minors. *The* major point is this: Satan is defeated. He was defeated temporarily in Christ's wilderness temptations. He was defeated eternally at Calvary. And he was defeated positionally when he launched his desperate, doomed counterattack that resulted in the loss of his privileged position of continuous access to God. The eviction notice has been served and executed. He won't be moving back into heaven for a resumption of his former 24/7 activity. For us this is good news, even great news. But this is also bad news. We'll see why tomorrow.

Through the Day

When we give attention to the enemy, we risk filling our minds with thoughts of him. The focus of our lives is Jesus who saved us and set us free. Satan is defeated. Celebrate that reality. Be alert to any attempt today to belittle a biblical belief in the enemy or to challenge the fact that he is defeated.

Evening Reflections

Did you meet any resistance today to your study of the truth about our enemy?

Did you recognize it for what it was?

Immediately? Later?

Our Way—Prayer

"My mighty King and loving Savior. How wonderful is the liberty You purchased for me. My life, my praise, is Yours alone. Your salvation is my helmet guarding my mind this night as I rest in Your care. Glory to Your name. Amen."

Week 3: Day 2
Our Enemy Is Dangerous

Our Weapon—His Word

(Read aloud.)

"Woe to the earth and the sea, because the devil has come down to you, having great wrath" (Revelation 12:12).

Beginnings

Pretending that a place or an activity is safe doesn't affect, in any way, the actual danger level of the place or practice. Acting as if the devil is just a man in a red suit with a pitchfork sweating away his days in subterranean magma caves does no one any good except the enemy himself. Be real. Stay alert. Our enemy is prowling around today with mayhem on his mind.

As missionaries from the African bush, our stateside assignment opportunities were always filled with blessings and not a few surprises and questions. One oft-repeated question, usually from a child, was "Did you see lots of lions and tigers in Africa?" My answer was always yes and no. Some of the places we lived in had good populations of lions but tigers were really hard to see since there aren't any in Africa!

As we look at today's focal Scripture (Revelation 12:12*b*), what is the first word? _____

Since this is a word rarely used in everyday conversation, what do you suppose it means? _____

_____

"Woe," used in this sense, is a word of exclamation signifying coming distress and grief.

Now read all of verse 12. "Rejoice" is the first operative word. The heavens and those there can celebrate. Satan's foul presence and critical tongue are history. But for earth and those of us here, there is a different word, "woe," and for good reason. Why are these days woeful for us? _____

_____

Satan's expulsion from heaven has ignited in him a rage that is not only murderous and unquenchable but intensified by a rapidly closing window of opportunity.

Look again at this week's key Scripture (1 Peter 5:8). What does Peter say our adversary, the devil, is doing?

_____

When lions aren't hungry, they don't prowl around, they lie around. (And I might add, nothing does "lie around" like a lion.) Our enemy is not lying around. He isn't even wandering around. He is intently on the prowl, his rage fueling vicious intent toward us, his intended prey.

Fearing tigers that don't exist is paranoid. Watching out for lions that do exist is wise. Our enemy is desperately dangerous. We always do well to heed Peter's warning,

"Be of sober spirit (stay steady, self-controlled), *be on the alert"*
(1 Peter 5:8).

Through the Day

What in your daily routine may be providing a portal of opportunity for the enemy? The music you choose? Checking the horoscope? Jokes you listen to or repeat? Pride? Gossip? An attitude toward others that you know is not God-pleasing? Web sites? Whatever, turn from it and be on guard against the one who hates you and schemes harm toward you.

Evening Reflections

Did God show you an area of your life where Satan was having his way?

Note it. Thank God for pointing it out and confess your turning from it.

Our Way—Prayer

"Thank You, Savior, for showing me something that shouldn't have been in my life and was giving the enemy an opportunity to weaken my walk with You and tarnish the reflection of You in me. All praise to You. Solidify and deepen the reality of this victory in me tonight and awake me to walk in greater fullness of Your life tomorrow. So let it be."

Week 3 Day 2

Week 3: Day 3
Our Enemy Is a Schemer

Our Weapon—His Word

(Read aloud.)

"Put on the full armor of God, so that you will be able to stand firm against the schemes of the devil" (Ephesians 6:11).

Beginnings

Jesus said, "I am the light of the world; he who follows Me shall not walk in the darkness" (John 8:12). Scheming, by its nature, goes on in the shadows. The enemy, who is the prince of darkness, loves the works of darkness like scheming. Begin today with the confession (aloud) that you are a child of the Light, a child of the King, and you will have nothing to do with any of the enemy's dark works.

Describe in your own words what a scheme is. _____
_____
Paul says (Ephesians 6:11) our aim is to (check one): (1) ____ stand firm against the enemy or (2) ____ stand firm against the schemes of the enemy.

It's Satan's schemes that we are to be on guard against. The word here translated "schemes" could also be accurately translated as the expert methods, the tactics, the traps, or the tricks of the enemy. Paul, in counseling the Corinthians, undergirds his counsel with the assurance that they know what they are talking about. "We are not ignorant of his [Satan's] schemes" (2 Corinthians 2:11). Satan, the commander in chief of the rebel forces opposing God and His love plan, is a master battle-field tactician. In his prowling about he sees weak points in our defenses, spies out possible avenues of attack, and then conceives plans.

Turn to Ephesians 4:14. As we are built up in the faith, maturing and growing in unity, what does Paul say we will no longer be as vulnerable to? _____

That's right. "False doctrine," "the trickery of men," and "craftiness in deceitful scheming." Walking in humility and responsiveness to Jesus results in our growing in wisdom and faith, rendering the enemy's scheming activities less effective.

We will understand Satan's character and ways better when we understand his names. The New Testament has a long list of names for the enemy. Let's look at four major ones. In Revelation 12:9 what are the four listed there? 1. _____ 2. _____ 3. _____ 4. _____

The last, and proper name, is Satan, which means "the adversary," "the opposer," "the one who accuses." Regardless of how Satan may try to make us think he is for us, he is not. He is always against us.

Then the devil. This word means "the slanderer." The devil's way is to speak false, derogatory things about us. Because of this we should not only recognize where painful lies told about us originate, we should also remember that when we speak slander, we are speaking the devil's language.

Next is the serpent. It was in the form of the serpent that Satan first stepped onto the stage of history as he came to Eve in the Garden of Eden. His role remains the same today. The serpent comes to deceive.

And finally, the dragon. It is in this expression that we see our enemy in his most terrible and terrifying form. He is a monster, vicious beyond reason. He prefers to portray himself as an angel of light (2 Corinthians 11:14) and his servants as servants of righteousness (2 Corinthians 11:15), but we know better. All of His plotting is with destructive intent.

When we speak slander, we are speaking the devil's language.

Through the Day

Knowing that our enemy is seeking to entrap us as we follow Christ, ask Jesus to point out to you any traps in your path today. Be alert to someone who may speak slanderous things about you. Stay secure in the One who loves you. His words to you and about you are words of love and affirmation. Praise Him.

Evening Reflections

Any struggles today? Tell them to the One who loves you and cares deeply. Note them here if you'd like.

Did the enemy try to trap you today? How did Christ alert you? How did you respond?

Our Way—Prayer

"Mighty Victor, I thank You for the victory of this day, walked out with You. You are great and greatly to be praised. Your plans, not the enemy's, were advanced today and I thank You."

Week 3: Day 4
Our Enemy Is a Liar

Our Weapon—His Word

(Read aloud.)
"Whenever he [the devil] speaks a lie, he speaks from his own nature, for he is a liar and the father of lies" (John 8:44).

Beginnings

Last week we mentioned that the battle always begins with truth. Why is it so important to understand our enemy's cornerstone strategy? Because he is, by nature, a liar and as such is always trying to deceive us. Today make sure you are living inside the surrounding defenses of truth. Believe no lies. First thing this morning, put on the belt of truth, that you may stand firm against his deceptive efforts. Ask God to show you any place your life is not lined up with His truth.

In today's focal passage (John 8:44), we have Jesus Himself revealing the essence of the moral character of our enemy, Satan. What two words does Jesus use to describe the devil? 1. _____
2. _____

Satan is, at heart, a liar and a murderer and we see this from our first historic encounter with him in the Garden. Look at Genesis 3:1 and following. We know from our study yesterday that the serpent and Satan are one and the same being. In looking here we also see immediately that he is "more crafty" than any other creature; and in this we find the source of the "craftiness in deceitful scheming" that Paul mentioned in Ephesians 4 concerning deceiving men. Deception is always Satan's primary strategy, humans are always the primary target, and casting doubt on what God says is always his primary means.

How did he begin his attack here? _____

_____

By seeming to quote God, he stimulated Eve's mental consideration while, at the same time, tempting her toward verbal engagement with him. What Satan said here is not exactly what God said, is it? Eve was right in her rebuttal but wrong in her effort. By taking the enemy's bait she was hooked. Meaning well, she allowed herself to be drawn into dialogue with the devil and, step by step, he advanced his strategy of turning her and her husband from God and thus spread his cosmic rebellion to earth. (Here we also discover a spiritual warfare principle: stay out of dialogue with the devil.)

> *Satan is, at heart, a liar and a murderer.*

Next, Satan arrogantly refuted God (Genesis 3:4: "You surely will not die!") and drew Eve further into his deception by offering a tantalizing, though false, reason for God's withholding of the fruit of the one tree. God wasn't good because He was withholding the best from her. Eve considered this, looked for herself (v. 6) and decided that it looked delicious (remember things are not always as they appear), was beautiful (the cliché that beauty is only skin deep really applies here and to anything from the devil), and definitely had drawing power (but so does a whirlpool and who wants to jump in one of those?). Despite knowing what the right decision was, she (and then Adam) rejected God and chose the lie (and thus the liar).

The result? Death. But that shouldn't have been any surprise. God had already told them that this would be the result if they ever disobeyed (Genesis 2:17). In this first episode of the enemy at work, we see clearly his nature as a liar and a murderer. He continues, to this day, to work straight out of his nature, using this same fundamental strategy.

Through the Day

We are surrounded by so much lying in life; ask Jesus to reveal today when someone is not telling you the truth. May He give you courage to speak to the person about the damage he or she is doing to his or her life. May God give you a deepened desire to walk in the truth.

Evening Reflections

What was the most significant thing that Jesus did in or through your life today?

Did you encounter any of the enemy's lies today? What?

Our Way—Prayer

"Lord of truth, I thank You that in You I know the truth and that truth has set me free from sin and death. How I thank You. My trust is in You, and in You do I rest. I bless You for that reality."

Week 3 Day 4

Our Weapon—His Word

(Read aloud.)

"The LORD has established His throne in the heavens, and His sovereignty rules over all" (Psalm 103:19).

Beginnings

As we have studied important truths about our enemy this week, it would not be a surprise to find that he has tried to stop those truths taking root in you by harassment, by sowing doubt, by bringing a cloud of oppression over you. This morning remember this truth from *Follow Me,* "The enemy cannot stand or stay where there is God-focused praise." Exalt the Lord Jesus. Declare His saving love for you. Praise His name. Confess His righteousness. And keep it up throughout the day.

God is sovereign. Satan is not.

Early in our first week of study we considered the power of perception and the enemy's efforts to make us think that the way things seem are the way things are. Billions of people (even if they are members of one of the world's major religions, including Christianity) practice some aspect(s) of a religion called animism. Animism is a belief that the world, both material and immaterial, is populated by spirits. Some of these spirits are good, but it is the "bad" ones we need to focus on. Understanding that there is evil out there (whether Satan himself is understood to be the source of it or not) these believers seek, in an infinitely varied number of ways, to appease malevolent forces with offerings and activities. This is the exact opposite of how God's Word teaches us to confront and deal with the devil and his evil spirits.

Read John 14:30. How does Jesus describe the devil? _____
_____

Now read 1 John 5:19. How is the world described in relation to the enemy? _____
_____

Satan is the ruler of the world and the whole world lies in his power. If we stopped right there, the perception would be that the animists have it right. The only way to deal with the devil is by appeasement. But we don't stop here. We look on.

Read today's focal verse, Psalm 103:19. How much does the word "all" encompass? (I know this may seem like a simplistic question but please answer it.) _____
"All" includes everything, doesn't it?

Now, what is sovereignty? _____
Sovereignty means to have supreme, preeminent power over. God is sovereign. His throne is established in the heavens, high above all, not just earth. He has supreme, preeminent power over earth and everything. That includes Satan and his forces. Satan doesn't want you to know that because he knows this: Truth trumps perception.

God is sovereign. Satan is not. Evil and evil activity do not originate with or emanate from God (they come from the father of lies), but they are under the sovereign authority of God *who works all things after the counsel of his will* (Ephesians 1:11). The most detailed example of this is found in the Book of Job, chapters 1 and 2. Here we see Satan pushing a destructive agenda against a God-fearing man named Job and how God ultimately determines what Satan will be allowed to do and the limits of his efforts. Regardless of how things may seem at times, Satan is not the master of the chessboard of life. God is.

Using all the equipment, walking and warring as God intends doesn't mean we will be immune to attack and pain. It does mean we will be victorious in it because God, not Satan, is in control.

Through the Day

Think on these truths as you walk through your day. God is sovereign. Satan is not. Worship the Lord, your Savior. Thank Him that all authority in heaven and in earth has been given to Him. He reigns! Nothing can come at you that has not been known by Him first and allowed by Him. Walk in that light, confident in Him.

Evening Reflections

As you think back over your day, what first comes to mind?

Was it a struggle with the enemy or the joy of walking in the truth? Or both?

Speak praise to Christ and resist the enemy knowing that God is working all things in your life according to the perfect plan of His will.

Our Way—Prayer

"Savior, I am so comforted by the reality of Your sovereignty. I rest in Your perfect wisdom and loving care. And I thank You that You are Lord, my Lord. Amen."

Strong Walk

Segue

Yesterday, as days often do, brought the surprise of what seemed to be a wholly incidental conversation with a man. The early conversation was surface, casual, and safe, but without warning the interior conversation, which is always ongoing in our lives, broke through into the open of our moment.

The setting was a porch swing. The timing, the transition from day to night when daytime's brilliantly intense backlight became "back-dark." Before us began to appear tiny points of light that we knew had been there all along. As you know, this is an overwhelming, humbling moment made possible every evening for those who have eyes to see.

Considering the stars stimulated the question, "Why did God stick us on this planet and keep us from being able to travel to all these stars and explore them?" This led to another question, "Why is it that every other celestial body that we know anything about is just dirt and rock and barren debris while earth is unique in its lushness and beauty?"

Honesty requires that the answers have to be, "We don't know." What we do know is that for some extended period of time heaven was a very unheavenly place as strife and dissension brought constant heartache (and I suppose headache as well) to God. Satan had already fallen from his exalted place to that of arrogant opposer when God decided to create the material universe that is our vast neighborhood and, as a key part of His master plan, put one small planet in it, perfectly balanced and intricately designed for the yet-to-be-created pinnacle of all creation, humans.

As majestic as the universe was, it didn't have fingerprints on it. It, with all its parts, had been spoken into being. The creation of this new being was the only thing that God created personally with His own hands. This had to have incensed Satan, the one who burned with power lust to elevate himself above God. Now there was actually a being hand-made by God, in the very image of God Himself, endued with the actual Spirit of God, enjoying intimate family fellowship with God. While Satan was fighting to get ahead, he was forced to admit that he was falling further behind. No wonder he desired to extend the range of his rebellion from the heavens to include this marvelous human home base, earth.

A generation ago, a popular American comedian named Flip Wilson (who also happened to be an unintentional theologian) managed to embed in the core beliefs of most Americans a new doctrine of accountability with a short toss-off line, "The devil made me do it." It never failed to get laughs but not from the heavenly audience. Popular culture had just validated an out for people. It wasn't their fault. It was the devil's. This belief morphed into other manifestations conveniently absolving us of all manner of responsibility in all manner of activity. How this plays out in the critical role of spiritual warfare is at least threefold: it distorts the actual, evil character of the devil by caricaturizing him; it blurs the critical self-understanding that we are responsible moral agents; and it opens the door (falsely) for other entities and agents to be shouldered with the blame for our sinful activity on earth.

As we move into the second part of this transformational pilgrimage as spiritual warriors, we must each understand and embrace the truth that no other person and no other thing is responsible for our thoughts and decisions and actions. Certainly earthly institutions and structures and places can have special spiritual significance and latent spiritual power, but biblically spiritual warfare is not primarily geographical or circumstantial or situational. It is moral.

The early church dealt with places of false worship and structures of oppression and bondage by calling those involved, whether perpetrators or victims, to decision. Turn from the wicked practices and beliefs and turn to the Savior. This does not preclude social ministry in Jesus's name but it does keep priorities lined up correctly. Human effort cannot change the heart. Only Jesus can. He is Truth and He alone can set us free and lead us in the right way, the true way (the moral way) to live. The New Testament is clear: Men and women overcame the evil one's high-place practices and low-life activities by obedience to Jesus and by witness of Jesus (Revelation 12:11). We are responsible agents of choice. Just as Eve could consider a wrong choice and make it, so could she, and so can we, consider right choices and make them.

At this point in the conversation, the man said, "There are times when I, as a Christian, know what is the right thing to do. But I still decide to do what is wrong because I want to. The bottom line is sometimes I want to do what I want to do, not what God wants done. What's going on? Why do I do this?"

In our next weeks of study, we will gain experiential understanding of some of the major ways that the enemy operates in the realms of the world and the flesh and his personal efforts against us. We will build a framework of understanding while developing godly habits that enable us to live free and victorious. Despite the enemy's activities, though, he is not to blame for our choices. We are responsible. Certainly he is always out to malign and deceive and ruin, but we are never at his mercy. We are not in his power. We are in Christ and we are living in His power.

The enemy's track record with God is terrible. No wins. All losses. Every one of his efforts against God and His Son have failed. His last and only opportunity is now all-out attack against us, the apple of our heavenly Father's eye. Satan knows the final outcome is fixed. He knows he can't win because he's already lost. But while he works to distract and destroy us, he also fights to hold on to as many of his captives as possible until it's too late for them. The Savior, though, is on a mission. He has come to set the captives free. We are some of those captives who have been set free. Stay free. Stand. Persevere. Resist—strong in the faith. And testify. A great host of the hopeless will be set free too. Hallelujah!

Fourth Week

Standing Firm Against Satan's Schemes:

In Person

K E Y   S C R I P T U R E

"That no advantage be taken of us by Satan, for we are not ignorant of his schemes" (2 Corinthians 2:11).

This week we will learn that Satan:

- Tempts
- Deceives
- Hinders
- Uses fortresses
- Demonizes

Our Weapon—His Word

(Read aloud.)

"And the tempter came and said to Him" (Matthew 4:3).

Beginnings

Knowing that there are realms of influence called the world and the flesh and that we have an enemy who operates personally in them with evil determination, start this new week armed and aware. Review the elements of your equipment as summarized on the last day of Week 2. Ensure that you are walking with them. Give particular attention to faith and the Word of God, two pieces of our armor which have special application to the personal actions of the enemy toward us. Express thanksgiving to God for His great gift of the Savior.

All of us have probably said at some point, "It was tempting, but I . . ." The temptation may have been a new car we couldn't afford or a doughnut we didn't need. All of us know the regular experience of being tempted. The two sides of temptation both work toward the same middle ground—sin. During the last week, we will study the other side of this dangerous issue of temptation—our side. Now we want to understand Satan's proactive part.

The first New Testament mention of our enemy occurs in Matthew 4. Read verse 1. Who leads Jesus into the wilderness? _____

_____

Yes, it is the Spirit of God.

And for what purpose? _____

_____

Reflected here is the truth we studied last week. (Satan is not sovereign, God is.) While the enemy may try to persuade us that he is working all things together according to his purposes, he's not. God is (Romans 8:28). God is using him for His purposes. Read Matthew 4:3. What name is given the enemy? _____

_____

From our first encounter with Satan (Genesis 3) to our first New Testament encounter with him, we see the same characteristic surfacing. He is the *tempter*. This word and its verb form (to tempt) are rooted in an old word meaning to try, to attempt, to experiment. Satan plots with purpose. He tries things that have high situational probability of working. (We'll see this in the first wilderness temptation.)

Mark this passage and turn to 1 Thessalonians 3:5. Why is Paul concerned about the Thessalonian believers? _____

_____

Despite solid foundational teaching and prophetic warning about coming affliction, there is danger that their faith may have wavered.

Who is the catalyst in this? _____

It is the same enemy again, Satan, the tempter. Cunningly, the devil takes real-life circumstances and plans temptations that can result in our faith failing.

Go back to Matthew 4. Looking at the first temptation, we see Jesus using faith and the Word of God to respond to Satan's attempt to get Him to sin. Read verses 3–4.

Jesus had been fasting for 40 days. The situation was primed for food to be a powerful temptation tool of the enemy's. Note, for our own application, these truths:

1. Jesus did not do what Satan wanted, but continued to do God's will.
2. Jesus did not look down to rocks for food, but continued looking up to God for His needs.
3. Jesus did not trust in His own power (He could turn the stones into bread), but in God's to accomplish

God is present. He has a plan. He will provide.

His purposes and deliver Him from the enemy's power at His right time.

4. Jesus recognized the real issue (trust in God), and reaffirmed it by quoting the Word of God.

Now read the second temptation (Matthew 4:5–7), and see a reversal in strategy.

Again for our own application:

1. Jesus was given into the enemy's hand for a time, but was not abandoned by God.
2. Satan tried to wrest the sword (the Word of God) from Jesus's hand by taking it and using it before Jesus did.
3. The devil wanted to make the Word the issue by tempting Jesus to test one of God's promises.

Again Jesus reaffirmed his faith in God by trusting in what He has said.

Read Matthew 4:8–10. Here Satan removes his mask and we see him as the evil (but temporary) ruler of this world.

Note and apply these truths to your own life:

1. Jesus is the rightful ruler of all the earth. Instead of the long, painful, and degrading road to the throne that God ordained, Satan offered a shortcut.
2. While it seems that Jesus would be serving in the role God intended, actually he would be serving Satan.
3. The temptation strikes at the cornerstone of God's law. We are to have no other gods before God. Jesus recognized the root of the temptation and rejected it, speaking the Word of God again.

And finally note the glorious truth of Matthew 4:11. God is present. He has a plan. He will provide. Always.

Through the Day

We see how critical it is that we know and stand in this truth: *"Resist the devil and he will flee from you."* The Holy Spirit has caused some of the truths that we discovered today to stand out as especially relevant to you. Look at those again before you walk through this day. Ask Him to keep you alert to the tempter's schemes.

Evening Reflections

Oh, how glorious it is to recognize the enemy's activity, to resist it, strong in the strength of the Lord Jesus.

What temptations did you encounter today?

How did you respond?

Our Way—Prayer

"You, O Lord, were faithful in all things that we might walk in Your victory. I thank You and praise You for the victories over the devil in my life today. Amen."

Week 4: Day 2
Our Enemy Deceives

Our Weapon—His Word

(Read aloud.)

"I am afraid that, as the serpent deceived Eve by his craftiness, your minds will be led astray from the simplicity and purity of devotion to Christ" (2 Corinthians 11:3).

Beginnings

Knowing that our enemy personally takes interest in our lives and plots to derail and wreck them, start today confessing the joyous reality of your salvation. You are loved with an everlasting love. You are accepted. God's wonderful salvation is a helmet that guards your mind from the doubts and deceptions by which the enemy would strike you. All praise to Jesus our wonderful Savior.

Have we not all met people whom we thought were wonderful, only later to discover they were not wonderful at all? We were encountering deceivers. Knowing that revelation of their real character would be unflattering, they pretend to be something else to deceive others and achieve their own goals. In today's focal verse, we see that the apostle Paul was gravely concerned that *the* deceiver, Satan, might do the same with believers in the Corinthian church. There was good reason for Paul's concern—the enemy had already deceived the whole world (Revelation 12:9).

Just as in the first deception he perpetrated (Genesis 3), Satan continues to make a cornerstone of his deceptions the casting of doubt upon what God says. For example, God says that sexual promiscuity and homosexuality are wrong (1 Corinthians 6:9–10). Satan says they aren't. The world, being deceived, rejects God and His truth, believes the lie, and calls them good, suffering the consequences. The same is true of lying, cheating, stealing, and on down the list. God has reasons for His laws and His reasons are always for our good.

You are loved with an everlasting love.

Satan, too, has reasons why he wants us to live in certain ways, but his reasons are *always* for our harm. This is a foundational truth that we must come to accept without question and stand solidly upon.

Look further into 2 Corinthians 11 to verse 14. What does Satan do regarding his appearance? _____

_____

Why would a person disguise himself? _____

_____

He doesn't want to be recognized. The same is true for Satan. He doesn't want us to recognize him. If people saw him for who and how he really is, very few would choose to follow him. Disguised as a powerfully attractive angel of light, he is able to deceive many into selfishly choosing the way of pain and damage.

Now read the fuller passage, 2 Corinthians 11:13–15. How does the devil usually do his work of deception? _____

_____

Sadly, it is through people who for their own purposes (and sometimes without full knowledge that they are actually servants of Satan) deceive others into rejecting God's plan for them and choosing the enemy's.

One day in our town, a motorcycle policeman making a traffic stop was struck and killed. The driver was not drinking or negligent in any way. When the investigation was complete, the cause was too simple to believe. Although it was daytime, the driver had not even seen the officer. And why not? She was blinded by the early morning light of the sun.

Satan, this false angel of light, is able to wreck lives by blinding people. How can we avoid being blinded and deceived? By making sure that we live each day encircled by the truth that always enables us

Week 4 Day 2

to see clearly. And then, by resisting the devil and trusting in Christ's righteousness (His pure goodness), which will make us eager to do what is right.

Through the Day

Be alert to ways that our enemy has been deceiving you. Ask the Lord Jesus to reveal these to you by His Holy Spirit. As He does, ask His grace and power to forsake them and walk in newness of life.

Evening Reflections

Think back over this day. What did Christ reveal to you?

What did the enemy try to do?

Were there any struggles?

Our Way—Prayer

"Dear Jesus, my Savior and the true and only Lord of Light. Thank You that Your Word is a light unto my path. Thank You that it was today. My heart is to follow You in the light. Help me, I pray. Amen."

Our Weapon—His Word

(Read aloud.)

"For we wanted to come to you—I, Paul, more than once—and yet Satan hindered us" (1 Thessalonians 2:18).

Beginnings

The One who called you saying, "Come, follow Me" is more than able to make that possible. There may be (and likely will be) hindrances to your obedience. Look to Him in faith, stand firm, and see how He clears the way.

My wife and I were waiting to check in at Boston's Logan Airport. The line, long and moving slowly, snaked back and forth inside the maze-maker fences. Directly behind us was a woman in her 30s who was becoming increasingly agitated at the slow pace of the line, the absence of agents behind the counters, and the confusion on the part of many travelers trying to use the electronic kiosk machines. At first, the woman just murmured to herself. Next, she began a verbal commentary on the stupidity of the travelers at the counters.

Then, unbelievably, she focused her frustration on the person at the head of the line. Although we were still far back, she began to shout over the crowd, "Number 2 is open. Go to number 2." Then, "What are you waiting on, man, go to number 7." And, "Hey, you. Don't you know what self-service means?" Finally, she left her luggage, ducked under several of the mobile fences, and went to the head of the line where she began to direct traffic. At this point, an airline employee came and taught her a bit about waiting in line. In the end, all of her complaining, fuming, criticizing, cursing, and generally making a fool of herself did not help her accomplish her goal of checking in any quicker. The only thing it hastened was the development of an ulcer.

Read our focal verse for today. What does Paul say Satan did regarding their desire to pay a ministry visit to the Thessalonian church?

_____

He hindered it. Read Romans 15:22. Paul was impeded from coming to the Romans for a long time and the reason (Romans 15:20)? Desiring to proclaim the good news of the Savior to those who had never heard he found himself continually hindered. Do we have any doubt who was hindering him?

How wonderful a shield faith is when hindrances and harassments come.

The same word is used in both passages. It can correctly be translated "thwart" or "hinder." Looking into its original usage has amazing insight for us as we come to a fuller understanding of what is going on when obstacles block our path of obedience to Christ. This word was used in military campaigns in regard to a foe who was losing. Because of this, he began to cut down trees across the road, burn bridges behind him, roll boulders into the way. But the purpose of all this effort was not to win It was simply to delay defeat.

While obstacles are not always from the devil, he does regularly seek to hinder our progress in the formation of Christ's life in us. He works to thwart our obedience and frustrate us. He works to delay his inevitable defeat.

We are told clearly in Scripture, "Be anxious for nothing" (Philippians 4:6). Instead of being anxious and frustrated what are we told to do? _____

As we look to the Lord with thanksgiving that He is working all things according to the counsel of His will, we can be at peace. Ask Him to grant grace and favor to respond to obstacles according to His character. Look to Him for guidance and power to deal with the hindrance. How wonderful a shield faith is when hindrances and harassments come.

Anyway, what's the hurry? We're called to walk. And He's promised to work.

Through the Day

It will be a rare day if there aren't hindrances from the enemy to your walking in faith.

Ask Christ to make you aware of the one behind these efforts and face them with patience and faith.

Evening Reflections

What hindrances did you encounter today?

How did you recognize them?

Were you able to respond to them without anxiety?

Our Way—Prayer

"Lord, You are the Prince of Peace. I know that the devil does not want me to know and follow You. I know he wants to thwart my obedience. I will not let that happen. I trust in You."

Week 4: Day 4
Our Enemy Uses Fortresses

Our Weapon—His Word

(Read aloud.)

"For the weapons of our warfare are not of the flesh, but divinely powerful for the destruction of fortresses" (*2 Corinthians 10:4*).

Beginnings

How beautiful is the truth that when we do what God says (for example in the stress of daily life, looking to Him in gratitude and petition instead of anxiety), His peace envelops us to a degree that we can't really understand or explain. This same peace actually becomes a defensive perimeter around our minds and hearts. Give Him the praise.

Since the 9/11 attacks, a new term has entered our national vocabulary: *sleeper cells.* Enemies of our nation no longer think of developing forces and weaponry to defeat us on the open field of battle. Instead, they've learned that great damage can be done and a whole nation crippled by small groups of devoted-to-the-death followers of a leader who is filled with rage and hatred. These hidden microgroups are known as sleeper cells.

Paul understands well that our enemy, the devil, developed this strategy long before twenty-first-century terrorists seized on it, and he refers to them as fortresses. Read 2 Corinthians 10:3–4 and let's note some key realities:

1. We do live "in the flesh," but we don't battle against our enemy with human strength. (v. 3)
2. We are adequately armed and this equipment is spiritual in nature, not physical (v. 4).

3. The purpose of our battlefield equipment is to destroy these fortresses (v. 4).

The word translated here "fortresses" and in other translations "strongholds" again is an old military word. In ancient times when one nation would occupy another, it would build stone fortresses at strategic locations and place a contingent of soldiers in them. Although the vast majority of the land would have no actual enemy forces in it, these relatively few occupied fortresses would be enough to put down resistance and continue control of the nation. The fortresses that Paul refers to in our lives operate in the same way. While usually few in number, they provide bases of operation for the enemy to exert his will in our lives and divert or quell any desires for freedom.

Read now 2 Corinthians 10:5. These fortresses are not constructed of stones. They are constructed of what? _____

_____

The building blocks of our enemy's fortresses are thoughts, thoughts that become patterns of thinking providing a place and a way for the enemy to exert control over our lives. What is it that Satan doesn't want us to have? _____

He knows that the more we know God, the more we will love Him and obey Him. So he raises up objections to what God requires, questions about what God says is right, doubts about God's love, resistance to God's plan, fear of God's ways, and on and on. The word translated "destroying" literally means to pull down. Satan raises up barriers. We pull them down. Each of these barriers is untrue thoughts about God. (Should we be surprised since Satan is a liar and the father of lies?) The barriers are fortresses for the enemy. So we take the truth and make sure we're surrounded by it, and then we take our mighty sword, the Word of truth, strike at the foundation of each of these barriers, and down they come.

> *The more we know God, the more we will love Him and obey Him.*

If left unaddressed, though, they give the enemy a place in our lives. Give him no place. Give him no quarter. Be ruthless at this point of impure, untrue, stray thoughts and impulses. Evict them by knowing and embracing the truth. Then lock the door of your mind and life, standing guard with that sword of the Word of truth. The thought is either consistent with the truth or is cut down.

Through the Day

Aware now of the reality of sleeper cells (fortresses) in the personal fabric of our lives, ask Jesus to begin a search-and-destroy mission in the earthly tent that is your body and life. This could be a long process. That's OK. Start today. Ask the Spirit to reveal lies that have taken root in your life and control some aspect of how you now live as a follower of the King. And remember: no rationalizations.

Evening Reflections

Write down what the Holy Spirit revealed to you today regarding untrue thoughts that have taken root in your mind and life and kept you from knowing God in growing fullness.

Our Way—Prayer

"King of kings, my life is not, and will not be a base for the enemy but a palace fit for You, *the* mighty Ruler of all and my King. Reign in me as I rest in You. Amen."

Week 4: Day 5

Our Enemy Demonizes

Our Weapon—His Word

(Read aloud.)

"While he was still approaching, the demon slammed him to the ground, and threw him into a convulsion. But Jesus rebuked the unclean spirit, and healed the boy and gave him back to his father. And they were all amazed at the greatness of God" (Luke 9:42–43).

A personal note: No day, no topic in this study has given me more pause than today's. Not because of reluctance to address the topic (it is critical), not because of fear (in Jesus we are perfectly protected), not because of disbelief in demons or their activities (they are present and active), but for these two reasons:

1. The inordinate amount of attention often given to this aspect of spiritual warfare can destroy a balanced view of spiritual warfare.
2. The immensity of the topic juxtaposed with the brevity of the space to address it.

The task is vitally important, and at the same time seemingly impossible. The goal today is to discover the key truths about demons and their activity in our lives so we can recognize them and resist them. But keep in mind that this is not a deliverance manual (entire books have been written on that topic) or a comprehensive study of either demonology or spiritual warfare.

Beginnings

Thank God that His Word is a lamp unto our feet and a light unto our paths that we might think and walk uprightly in His sight. He is the One who can keep us straight in the exciting process of trying to maintain our balance.

An incident occurred during President Jimmy Carter's administration that could have had serious international ramifications. In discussions with Soviet officials, President Carter spoke of the importance of continuing intercourse between the two nations. In translation, unfortunately, a Russian word having sexual connotations was chosen instead of the correct one reflecting verbal dialogue. It was an embarrassing day for America, but it pointed up an important truth: Make sure you say what you mean.

The primary word used in the New Testament for the activity of demons in people is translated in the King James Version of the Bible as well as a number of other translations as "demon possessed." However, the original Greek word used in all of these passages has no connotation of possession. What the word really means is "demonized."

Recently our county commissioners voted to pay thousands of dollars to a couple for a narrow strip of land where a disputed road currently runs. The reason? The couple has possession of the land that the road lies on and determining who actually owns it would be a long, messy, and expensive process. In normal circumstances, a possession is something that is yours and the commissioners decided it was best to operate on that premise.

Demons are evil, unclean spirits who do Satan's bidding. From Scripture and through confirming experience, it seems that there are three primary ways that demons affect people (i.e., demonize them).

First is what we would normally describe as *control* of nonbelievers. Read Mark 5:1–16. From this episode we can draw some important conclusions:

1. It's clear that a person can be effectively controlled by demons.
2. Nowhere in Scripture, though, is there an example of a believer being possessed by demons.
3. Control by demons can result in horrible injury to and abuse of the person.

(See also Matthew 17:14–18 and 15:22–28.)

Secondly, demons can affect or afflict all people, believers and non-believers alike, through deception and harassment. Read 1 Timothy 4:1. Here Paul states the reality that demons can affect believers by drawing their attention away from the truth and influencing them to turn from continuing in the faith. We also know through biblical examples (King Saul, 1 Samuel 15 and 16) that when we rebel against God, evil spirits can come and torment. We also know this from observing demonized people today.

And thirdly, there is the reality of demonic presence and deceptive influence *in* believers. This reality brings perhaps the greatest dispute, but must not be dismissed just because there is disagreement. Turn to 1 John 4:4. Who do we belong to? _____ And the Spirit in us is __ more powerful or __ less powerful than the spirit in the world. When we invited Jesus to be the Lord of our lives, God removed us from the kingdom of darkness and transferred us to the kingdom of Christ (Colossians 1:13). Thus believers cannot belong to the enemy and cannot be controlled or possessed by him. They can, however, have demons that still attach themselves to areas of our human lives, sin being a major point of entry, and negatively influence aspects of our lives. The fortresses (strongholds) that we studied yesterday are the base of operations for these demonic deceptions.

Through the Day

More fully aware of the place that demons play in either controlling or harassing people, celebrate your life in Christ today. Invite Him to continue His work of transformation and guard against any sin that could provide fertile soil for demonic activity.

Evening Reflections

As you reflect back on this day, have you seen any evidences of the demons of our enemy at work?

In what ways?

Our Way—Prayer

"Lord Jesus, You reign. I lift You up as Lord of all. I want You to reign in all areas of my life and I invite You to do that. My trust is in You. My rest is in You. Be exalted."

Fifth Week

Standing Firm Against Satan's Schemes:

In the World

"And the great dragon was thrown down, the serpent of old who is called the devil and Satan, who deceives the whole world" (Revelation 12:9).

<u>*This week we will learn that Satan deceives through:*</u>

- Models
- Media
- Values
- Ambitions
- Relationships

Week 5: Day 1
Satan Uses Models

Our Weapon—His Word

(Read aloud.)

"And do not be conformed to this world, but be transformed by the renewing of your mind" (Romans 12:2).

Beginnings

Today, as every day, we will be surrounded by forces seeking to get us to conform to someone else's desires for us. The first step in this process is always the same: getting us to think about the change. Bow now and thank God that you have the mind of Christ. Declare that you want His thoughts to be your thoughts all day and ask His help as you guard your mind.

Pencil-thin, she appeared without fanfare in the 1960s. Certainly she had to be the most unlikely of candidates to impact a whole era. Nevertheless, from the first time she moved down the fashion runway, the herd was captivated. Although her real name is lost to history, her moniker (and her influence) endures: Twiggy. Decades later women are still bombarded by thoughts of inadequacy and distress because they believe they aren't thin enough.

A woman whose job it is to display new clothes at a fashion show is just one example of a model. In its fullest sense, a model is an example that becomes a standard to compare to and then imitate.

Recently I read of a new social phenomena known as CWS (celebrity worship syndrome). The report stated that as many as one-third of Americans manifest this condition and thus have their thoughts and lives significantly controlled by it. Considering that celebrities in our country are rarely good role models and already as many as one-third of Americans are mentally and emotionally obsessed with them, we can quickly see the destructive avenue our enemy has with which to harm our lives.

List some things that you have seen in the last few days that were presented as models.

1.

2.

3.

Were these models good ones? Yes _____ No _____

How do you know?

Open your Bible to Acts 17:10–12. When the Bereans encountered a new model for thinking and living, how did they judge its merits?

_____

The example of the Bereans is an excellent model for us in our daily living.

1. They understood that you must have a standard against which to measure new influences.
2. They knew that not all things are true or good.
3. They were diligent, daily measuring these new influences against the reliable standard.
4. When they had made their determinations, they chose to accept what was true according to the Scriptures and reject what wasn't.

As we reflect on their guiding principles, is it any wonder the Bereans are described as noble-minded?

It would be difficult to count how many times in one day we are faced with models that are put forward as good and "a delight to the eyes." Yet the point is not the number, but the unceasing flow of them. Accept that Satan is constantly parading unhealthy models across our path for the purpose of stimulating our minds to conform to the world.

Week 5 Day 1

What part of our armor is essential to repulsing these efforts? _____

_____

That's right. It is truth. God's truth encircling us like a belt, protecting us at the center of our being. We keep belting on His truth by doing just what the Bereans did: make every new tempting example take the truth test. If it doesn't pass, reject it. You will find that rather than being *"conformed to this world,"* you will be *"transformed by the renewing of your mind."*

Through the Day

As you prepare to move into your day, first bow and ask God to alert you to the enemy's conforming efforts as you encounter them.

Evening Reflections

What models did you encounter today that were held up as attractive examples for you to embrace?

In recognizing them for what they are—the enemy's efforts to get us to conform to the world's ways—did you recognize any that you had already allowed into your life?

If so, what?

Did you forsake them?

Our Way—Prayer

"Father, thank You that truth transforms. And thank You for revealing to me today models that the enemy was trying to use to conform me to the world. I reject them and rejoice that Jesus is my example and I want to be conformed to His image."

Week 5: Day 2

Satan Uses Media

Our Weapon—His Word

(Read aloud.)

"The lamp of the body is the eye. If therefore your eye is good, your whole body will be full of light" (Matthew 6:22).

Beginnings

Now that you are more aware of how the enemy uses pervasive societal models to divert our attention and then reshape our thoughts, begin this new day with thanks to God that you have the Spirit of Christ dwelling in you. Invite Him to fill you afresh so that you can discern between good and bad influences today. Thank Him that He will, and praise Him that He always is our best example.

In the 1970s when tennis was "hot" in America and my wife and I were young marrieds, we often played both singles and doubles. During this period, I noticed something that I could never quite explain. We were both average players; but when we watched a tennis tournament on television and then went to the courts, we always played better. It didn't make sense, but it was true. It took 30 years for me to realize why. Coaches and trainers now know that by having athletes repeatedly watch the correct way to swing or move, they will more easily duplicate it when they take the field to practice. In other words, when first the mind is trained, the body then more readily follows.

Often the blame for the moral decline of our nation is laid on "the media." Having come this far along this transformational path, we already know that is not true. We are the ones responsible for our choices and actions. The word *media* is just the plural form of the word *medium,* and a medium is simply a means of communication. Like any tool, these means are powerless to accomplish anything. Their impact is determined first by content and then by usage.

Look at Jesus's words in Matthew 6:22–23. What metaphor does Jesus employ here? _____

Looking at a home that we were considering purchasing, I flipped on the light switch in a room and nothing happened. A little investigation revealed the problem. The light switch wasn't actually a light switch. Instead, it sent power to an outlet in the room. To have light in that room you needed to plug in a lamp. Jesus illustrates here that our eyes function as lamps for our lives. What we plug into determines what kind of light streams into our lives. And the outlets? The most easily accessible ones today are media outlets.

> *We are the ones responsible for our choices and actions.*

There is no argument that much (probably most) of what is streamed across our field of vision today through the media is very poor light with which to light a life. The fact that this is out *there* doesn't mean that it has to come in *here.* The point of entrance is the eyes. And we control them, don't we?

Critical to stripping away the opportunity that we daily give the enemy to darken our lives is recognizing that much media content is "another gospel." Its result is not light and life but darkness and death. Just as a pipe can be used to bring clean water and health to a home, so it can also be used to carry sewage and sickness. Repetitive exposure to what is inconsistent with godliness trains our minds and thus makes it easier for our bodies to then follow. *"If your eye is bad, your whole body will be full of darkness"* (Matthew 6:23 NKJV).

Our salvation, our right standing with God because of faith in Jesus, our Savior, functions as a helmet protecting our minds and thus our lives. It means we are no longer slaves to sin. We are free to choose to walk in the light that is this salvation relationship with God and live free. Satan knows that steady exposure to his messages has the potential to influence and then recondition the mind, to darken it. He delights that the perfect media and environment for this exist in our day. From television in nearly every home (which I've read is on for seven hours a day in the average American home) to radios in our cars, and now even on our heads as we walk or jog, to magazines in our mailboxes and waiting rooms and along every checkout line: all can repeatedly train our minds to sin so that our bodies then will follow.

Through the Day

Today, resist the enemy and his nonstop barrage, firm in your faith. You are not at the enemy's mercy. You are under God's great mercy. Remember, *"If . . . your eye is good, your whole body will be full of light."*

Evening Reflections

To what media were you exposed today?

What ungodly messages and images did you encounter through them?

How did you reduce or eliminate their entrance into your mind and thus your life?

Our Way—Prayer

"Savior, thank You for opening my eyes to the pervasiveness of the enemy's evil efforts to turn my thoughts and thus my life away from the way of truth and life. As I lie down to rest this night, may Your Spirit speak peace and truth to me that I might rise tomorrow to walk in newness of Your life. Thank You."

Our Weapon—His Word

(Read aloud.)

"Do you not know that friendship with the world is hostility toward God?" (James 4:4).

Beginnings

"Father, Your Word lights the way that I should walk today. Thank You that I don't have to wonder or to wander. I choose to look to You and listen to You. Guard my mind today, I pray."

In the 2004 national elections the press was stunned by the emergence of the so-called values voter. A significant number of Americans made their choices for leaders based not on what they believed was best for themselves personally but what they believed was best for the country, and their votes decided the election. Values, those ideals that affect how we think and live, were always present; but suddenly, it seemed, they had come out of hiding and in a big way.

Living overseas as missionaries in the 1970s and 1980s, we were disconnected from the abortion debates that went on in our country. When we returned here, I was dismayed to find that while the majority of Americans believed (and still do) that the killing of babies before birth was wrong, they still said it was all right to do it. How could this be? Values determine decisions. Always. For years I lived with this dilemma until one day, serving on a task force unrelated to this topic, a member mentioned research that indicated that the number one value in America was choice. I don't remember what the relevance of that statement was to our working context that day because my mind instantly (and finally) saw clearly why we as a people could say one thing (i.e., abortion is wrong) but endorse the other. The lives of children, especially those of the smallest and most helpless, were of lower value than personal preference.

Values always determine behavior. When we deny that, it is because we don't want to admit that we have actually elevated another value above what we say or what we think we value most. Our enemy understands well the power values hold over people and works to bring pressure on us, usually in attractive and subtle ways, to adopt values consistent with his purposes.

When a starlet or talk show host lives openly in sin with a man and seems to prosper in spite of it, millions of women and girls are tempted to think that they can do the same without harm. The "star's" personal values bring widespread harm across a nation by stating, through example, that she knows better than God how to best live.

When a business or real estate mogul models greed as good, his or her example is beamed at us through best-selling books, front page newspaper stories, prime-time TV shows, evening entertainment reports, and even a closed-circuit monitor in Wal-Mart! The way of richest living is not to "lay up treasures on earth." God tells us that. Everything is God's and He intends us to be careful keepers of it. Instead, though, we lust to gather everything we can, anyway we can. Then, contrary to the promise, we adopt the world's values only to discover that our lives are not richer but sadder.

Values always determine behavior.

Open your Bible this morning to the Old Testament Book of Judges 17:6. What does God state about the situation among His covenant people?

_____

Now turn to the end of the book and read the last words (Judges 21:25). What is God's final commentary of this era of His people?

_____

Try to make time this weekend to read all that is recorded between these two verses.

Watch for these truths.

Without godly leadership the people continue to turn from the central values of a people of God—fidelity to Him in faith and obedience to His directives in life—to their own.

This self-centeredness expresses itself, as it always does, in self-assertion.

Self-assertion reveals that it's always governed by self-interest.

And the consequences of this scenario? Ludicrous behaviors are rationalized because of long-eroded values resulting in chaos, violence, and finally disintegration of society.

In other words, when God is not the ultimate value in our lives, our values and then our actions will be governed by what we believe is right in our own eyes, not what is right in His eyes. Our enemy knows this and works tirelessly to lead us to the position.

Only righteousness builds up a nation (Proverbs 14:34). In accepting Jesus, He gave us His righteousness, and His righteousness enables us to live righteously.

Through the Day

The Holy Spirit may have already illumined to you this morning a worldly value that you have allowed the enemy to work into your life. Before you even think of beginning your day's work, bow and repent of this. Then ask God to sharpen your sight to see other values that are under attack in your life.

Evening Reflections

What did the Holy Spirit reveal to you today?

Have you found compromise in some of your values? Where?

Our Way—Prayer

"Gracious God, I confess that Your ways are best—absolutely. Thank You for revealing to me the unrelenting pressure on me from the enemy to compromise Your values in my life. I declare my rejection of him and embrace You in love this night."

Week 5 Day 3

Week 5: Day 4
Satan Uses Ambitions

Our Weapon—His Word

(Read aloud.)

"Therefore also we have as our ambition, whether at home or absent, to be pleasing to Him" (2 Corinthians 5:9).

Beginnings

Today, whether you consciously recognize it or not, you will be encouraged to go after what you want, pushing forward to get ahead of others. Diligence and drive are not necessarily bad. Just be sure today that your drive is directed toward pleasing Christ in what you do. Be on guard for the enemy's efforts to subtly redirect your efforts.

"Lord Jesus, You are the One I love and want to follow. Help me."

Values line the road. Ambition drives us down it.

In the cities of America, traffic helicopters guide rush hour by seeing the Big Picture and suggesting alternate routes to frustrated drivers. In navigating life, there are many roads to choose from; and without Big-Picture guidance, we risk taking the wrong road and suffering the consequences. This risk is exacerbated by the fact that we are not passive passengers in this journey. We're behind the wheel, doing the driving, making the decisions.

Today, to this foundational truth, we add an important additional dynamic: We are driving but we're also driven. Latent in us is an earnestness to achieve. When this is activated and then linked with a willingness to work, we have something called ambition (or as it is often described—drivenness). Ambition or drivenness is good as long as it is balanced and the direction is right.

Looking at today's scriptural focus, what is the center line of the road God intends us to travel down? _____

_____

Indeed it is pleasing Him. Knowing the right direction is first in importance. When I am traveling to a new location, the first thing I do is use Mapquest to get directions to the destination address. This is important, but it is not my goal. My ambition is to get where I need to go. The question then becomes: Can I and will I follow the directions? In America today, there is growing consternation among Christian leaders. Research is revealing that church members know what is right but are increasingly not doing it. We know the way to live, but selfish ambitions cause us to choose alternative values that are producing detours in our travel. We must remember that our enemy lines the alternate routes of life with signs displaying values that are consistent with his purposes and attractive to our own ambitions. And the result?

Turn to Proverbs 16:25. _____

The way *seems* right but the result shows that it is not.

Let's consider a couple of examples:

For some of you it may be springtime as you walk through this study. April 15 is approaching and you are working on your taxes. You're realizing your bill is going to be more than you want to pay. As you stand at that crossroad, considering which way to go, the enemy shows you a side path marked by a value sign that reads, "Everyone cheats on their taxes." You know that God is watching (although you may not want to think about that) but the IRS isn't (although they might come back later and take a look). An ungodly ambition (greed) joined with an enemy-installed validating value (i.e., everyone cheats on their taxes) presents a dangerous temptation. Which road will you take? You know the right direction, but that is not the goal. Choosing it is.

Walking into your office building, a co-worker mentions something she heard about you that would hurt your chances of getting that promotion for which you've worked so hard. You know instantly who started the false rumor. You want to get back at him and you see down a side street a sign (value) that reads, "Do unto others as they do unto you." You feel justified and want to act on the validated impulse, but then you are reminded of what God values: "Do unto others as you would *have them* do unto you." You face a choice.

Of critical importance—When we realize we have gotten on the wrong road, we must not think, "Oh, well, I'll just have to make the best of it." No. We have to turn around and go back where we made the wrong turn and get on the right road again. By doing this, we turn our backs on the values that line that wrong way and put godly values again in front of us. In doing this, we are resisting the devil. When we do this, what does he do? (James 4:7)

That's right. He turns and runs from us. This is the kind of walk that keeps the enemy on the run.

Through the Day

Ask God to reveal to you today any ambitions that may be consistent with Satan's values and not God's. As He does, stop immediately and repent. If you find yourself trying to ignore His illumining, confess that Jesus is your Lord and ask His help to make the course corrections that He deems necessary.

Evening Reflections

Where today did you recognize that you have been driven by a selfish, ungodly ambition that pleases you but not Christ?

What was your first response to this?

Our Way—Prayer

"Lord Jesus, I'm tired of the stress and frustration of trying to live the world's way. I want to live Your way. Continue to strive with me and give me help to walk more and more back into the way that is pleasing to You and peaceful to me. Thank You."

Our Weapon—His Word

(Read aloud.)

"For our struggle is not against flesh and blood" (Ephesians 6:12).

Beginnings

Responding rightly depends upon seeing clearly. Pray, "Lord, You are the only One who sees everything clearly and correctly. I need your sight and your insight. As I walk with people today, guide me by Your Spirit that I may resist the evil one and respond to You and to people as You would have me to."

Probably nothing in life is more difficult, and causes greater pain, than interpersonal relationships, whether it's simple office tension or nations going to war against each other. On the surface it seems obvious—people are the problem. But could the real issue be deeper than that? Our focus Scripture today gives us a clear word on this question—contrary to appearances, people alone are *not* the problem. Wrestling with difficult, even mean people, one must recognize that someone else likely is involved as well.

> Who is really at work in this situation?
> How does God want to work in it?

Let's seek the answer to the first question. Turn to Ephesians 2:2. When people aren't obeying God, doing the opposite of what He says and living the way the world lives, who is actually working in them?

It is indeed the one who is always in opposition to God and His ways of life. It is Satan.

Before we knew Christ as our loving Savior, we knew no other way to live. We were locked in sin, living just like the world lives. The devil had a heyday working his will in our lives. But when we were set free, he lost his grip. The "spirit . . . now working in the sons of disobedience" was no longer the controlling spirit working in us. The Spirit of peace and liberty was. And He is the Spirit of Jesus, our Savior. Now we cannot only recognize a right choice, we have the power to make it and benefit from it. One of the greatest benefits is this: choosing the Prince of Peace brings peace with God and the amazing potential of peace with others.

Disobedience always delights the devil and damages our lives.

How does God want to work in us in tense, even hostile relationships? He wants us to pursue peace (Hebrews 12:14).

If someone has something against us, whether rightly so or not, Jesus wants us to go and seek reconciliation (Matthew 5:23–24). As difficult as this is when we have been the offending party, it is even harder when the other person is the offender against us. Worldly thinking would expect the other person to come to us, but that isn't the way of Christ's kingdom. God works through those who are at peace with Him to bring peace on this earth. We are His ambassadors. When we obey Him, we strip away the enemy's opportunity to advance his divisive, destructive work.

Remember this truth: Wherever we are disobedient, we are giving the enemy opportunity to continue his evil work in our lives. Disobedience always delights the devil and damages our lives.

A sad reality in interpersonal relationships is that sometimes a person may refuse to reconcile. Do not, out of ignorance, give the devil an advantage when this happens by feeling that you are doomed to a strained relationship with God because of another's hard heart. God is very clear. As far as it depends on us, we are to be at peace with everyone (Romans 12:18). Just make sure that this is the case and then continue to keep your heart open to God so that nothing disturbs your peace.

How should we respond to the person who remains at odds with us? Turn to Luke 6:27–28 for Jesus's instructions on this point.

For the one who continues as an enemy we are to _____ him.

For the one who hates us, we are to _____ to him.

For the one who curses us, we are to _____ him.

And for the one who continues to mistreat us, we are to _____ for him.

By doing this, we give God every opportunity to break through into that life. We also deny the enemy an opportunity. That's the way it should be.

Through the Day

Today may very well be the start of a painful period. Whenever the reality of broken relationships is surfaced we face a great danger of rationalizing our way around God's clear commands. Set yourself to flat-out reject this path. Instead, surrender yourself to His lordship and invite Him to begin to set you free from relationship bondages through explicit obedience to Him.

Evening Reflections

Did you find resistance, even refusal, rising up in you today as the Holy Spirit sought to lead you into obedience?

How did you respond? (It is critical that you be completely honest at this point.)

Our Way—Prayer

"Father, You know that I don't want to pray tonight. I want justice. But even as I say that, I know that You are a just God and in Your time You will bring justice. For now You want to bring me peace. Help me to want that, too, to want it so much that I will let You work it Your way in me. I need Your help."

Sixth Week

Standing Firm Against Satan's Schemes:

Through the Flesh

K E Y   S C R I P T U R E

"Keep watching and praying that you may not enter into temptation; the spirit is willing, but the flesh is weak" *(Matthew 26:41).*

This week we will learn how Satan uses:

- Desires of the flesh
- Desires of the mind
- Temptation
- Unforgiveness
- Impatience and anxiety

Week 6: Day 1
Guarding Against the Flesh

Our Weapon—His Word

(Read aloud.)

"But I say, walk by the Spirit, and you will not carry out the desire of the flesh. For the flesh sets its desire against the Spirit" *(Galatians 5:16–17).*

Beginnings

Paul made plain that the way we lived before we knew the Savior was by continuously *"indulging the desires of the flesh and of the mind"* (Ephesians 2:3). As we enter this last week, let's reject again the ubiquitous message of our age and our world, which is "indulge yourself." Instead, determine to live out Christ's words, *"If anyone wishes to come after Me, he must deny himself"* (Luke 9:23). Knowing how hard this is, bow in prayer, asking Him to deepen your understanding to the reality of His victory over the flesh and the devil and our practical, moment-by-moment place in that victory.

A Brazilian friend and I were talking about life in his country when the subject of Carnival came up. Each year in Brazil a multiday, 24/7 street party is held throughout the nation. The world portrays Carnival as a glorious time, the high point of the year; but, in truth, Carnival is unbelievable as nudity, drunkenness, and immorality are paraded in the streets (its counterpart in the USA is Mardi Gras in New Orleans and increasingly other Gulf Coast cities). The word *carnival* means a celebration of the flesh. The irony of it is that this time of profligate indulgence is directly linked to the start of Lent, the annual season of penitent sorrow for sin and self-denial through fasting. The apostle Paul agreed that we should celebrate (Romans 7:25), but the celebration is over the glorious reality that Jesus Christ our Lord has set us free from slavery to the flesh.

Before we open our Bibles this morning, we *must* pause, bow again, and thank God for the answer to Paul's (and our) heart-cry question, *"Wretched man* (or woman) *that I am! Who will set me free from the body of this death?"* (Romans 7:24). Thank God right now. Jesus is the One!

When we place our trust in the Savior, we are grafted into Christ who is the True Vine (John 15). Paul knew this. In fact, a classic book about the apostle Paul is titled *A Man in Christ.*

Open your Bible to 2 Corinthians 5:17. Anyone who is "in Christ" is what? _____

That individual is a new person. All of the "old" is history. The old nature is dead, having been put to death with Christ (Romans 6). The person now has a new nature, Christ's nature. This is critical to victory over the flesh. We do not have our old, sinful nature. We have a new one that opens the door to our living a life pleasing to God. In Jesus we actually have the power to live in that new nature. It can be done.

Turn to Romans 6:11. What reality are we now to accept? _____

_____

Romans 6:12. In light of this reality, what are we to do? _____

_____

Romans 6:13. What are we to stop doing and now start doing? ____

_____

We must not let sin have its way in our lives any longer. As believers we learn quickly that while this reality is true it doesn't often seem true. We seem to be unable to actually put into practice what we know we must. When we respond to the desires and demands of the flesh, we realize two things: (1) we're falling victim to schemes of the enemy and (2) we are opening our lives to his further schemes. What are we to do?

Look at Romans 8:11. We know what to do. Here's how we can actually do it.

Jesus' Spirit, who now lives in us, will give us everything we need to live free.

We have all we need. Keep believing that. Keep striving mightily against sin. Keep asking for His strength and power. He will give it. Thank God.

Week 6 Day 1

We have a friend who had two cats. She was the perfect pet owner, loving and caring for her cats. But when she wasn't watching, they would shred her drapes and destroy her furniture with their claws. She had two options: have the cats declawed or constantly be vigilant and stop them whenever they tried to do what came naturally.

Unfortunately, when it comes to the flesh, we don't have the first option. We can't have it declawed. But we do have the second option and we can be successful if we are on guard, depending on Christ's power to be victorious.

Through the Day

It's very important today that you take Jesus's Word to heart:

"Keep watching and praying that you may not enter into temptation; the spirit is willing, but the flesh is weak" (Matthew 26:41).

Before heading out into the world today, in faith, ask His help. He will give it.

Evening Reflections

Where did He show you that you were giving in to the flesh?

Was it an area of habitual sin?

Did you turn from it and ask His forgiveness and help to no longer participate in it?

How did Jesus help you in a particular situation today?

Our Way—Prayer

"Lord Jesus, I know that I am not to give my mind and my body to be instruments of sin; but I also know it has been so hard not to. As I go to sleep tonight, I consciously, intentionally, turn from this practice that has gone on far too long in my life and commit myself to look to You in faith for power to resist, reject, and refuse the demands of the flesh and the enemy tomorrow. Thank You."

Week 6 Day 1

Week 6: Day 2
The Battlefield of the Mind

Our Weapon—His Word

(Read aloud.)

"For the mind set on the flesh is death, but the mind set on the Spirit is life and peace, because the mind set on the flesh is hostile toward God; for it does not subject itself to the law of God" *(Romans 8:6–7).*

Beginnings

In Week 4 of our study we saw how important a base of operations inside a person was to the enemy's influence over that person's life. Today we look at the same issue from our perspective. We know that Satan has gained some degree of control when he gets inside a person's mind, and so he plots to accomplish this through something called the desire of the mind. Bow this morning and declare the truth that in Jesus we have the mind of Christ (1 Corinthians 2:16). Invite the Lord of all, Jesus, the One who loves us, to inhabit your mind and fashion it to reflect His.

For centuries, enemy armies invaded areas, moving freely about as they sought to conquer other peoples. The residents knew that they couldn't keep these armies from roaming the countryside, but they could keep them out of their cities. Their freedom and their very lives depended on this. They defended their cities by building and then mounting guards on strong walls. From this we can draw a principle for our own warfare:

> Often you can't keep the enemy out of the 'hood
> but you can keep him out of the house.

These early defenders also knew something that we have forgotten: you can't let the enemy into the house and expect life to be what you want it to be (and the ultimate "want" is for liberty). The very idea of peaceful coexistence with the enemy was ludicrous to them and it should be to us.

Since both sides knew that rarely could defensive walls be breached, the special focus of both the enemy's offensive strategy, as well as the defender's fortification and defense, was at the gates, which allowed both entrance and exit. (Today we focus on the entrance function; tomorrow on the exit aspect.) Block the enemy at these points and life inside was secure.

Wisdom is right application of right knowledge.

Read Romans 7:14–23. Here Paul delineated the dilemma we all face as new-nature creations in Christ living in old-nature bodies. What did Paul say about the flesh (Romans 7:18*a*)? _____
_____

The flesh is not good.

And what about our dilemma? _____
_____

The "wishing" to do right is present but the actual doing of it is not.

So where is this battle going on and thus where can it be won? (Romans 7:22–23) _____

"The law of the mind" is godly wishing and willing struggling with ungodly desires of the mind and the flesh. But knowing of this struggle does not automatically translate into victory in the struggle. That's what Paul is crying out about here. Wisdom is right application of right knowledge. First, we need knowledge of the situation; but then we need to know how to rightly apply it if we are to live wisely and victoriously. And here is the way.

Look at 2 Corinthians 3:5*b*. Where does our adequacy for this, or any endeavor as a believer, come from? _____
_____

It comes only from Him. As Paul so poignantly describes, even when we desperately want to live godly in Christ, we can't. We keep doing the very things we know not, and don't want, to do. In resisting the devil and walking strongly in the Spirit of Christ (Galatians 5:16), we are empowered to live victoriously.

At a conference some years ago, I heard John Piper relate an experience that illustrates this point. Just before he went out to mow the lawn, someone had told him of a particular sexual sin they had glimpsed. As Piper began to mow, he realized that a graphic picture of this act was beginning to root in his mind. He instantly resisted the thought, declaring it under the authority of Christ and demanding it depart from his mind. It did. But as he went back and forth mowing the grass, the battle went back and forth. The enemy, knowing the sinful desire of the mind and the flesh, kept trying to come into his life through these particular gates, forcing the mental picture back inside. Piper, laboring together with Jesus and from his new nature (1 Corinthians 3:9*a*), kept resisting it, pushing it back out. Eventually the enemy did just what God said he would: he left (James 4:7).

The desire of the mind stands ready to betray the city that is our lives by meeting the enemy at the gate with a key. Knowing this we keep the gates of our lives strong and guarded. When an effort is made to invade, we resist it and keep on rejecting it in the power of Jesus until defeat is assured.

Again, this is the kind of walk that puts the enemy to flight.

Through the Day

The Spirit may already have shown you gates in your life where enemy advances are meeting up with ungodly desires. Thank God right now for making you aware of that. Ask for and depend on His almighty strength as you reject these thoughts and root them out of your mind and life.

Specifically now, pray, "Lord Jesus, You are my life. All my adequacy for everything is found in You. Apart from You, out there on my own, I can't be victorious. I look to You right now and ask Your grace and power to bring every thought into submission and conformity to Your desires. Thank You. Thank You."

Evening Reflections

Was today a difficult day?

In what way?

How did Jesus meet you and help you as you looked to Him in faith?

Our Way—Prayer

"Master, how I can relate to Paul's struggle with the desires of the mind and of the flesh. Thank You that today I tasted victory. You are the victory. You are my victory. You give me Your victory in these struggles. I lie down now to rest in You. Guard my mind. Thank You."

Week 6 Day 2

Week 6: Day 3
The Other Side of Temptation

Our Weapon—His Word

(Read aloud.)

"But each one is tempted when he is carried away and enticed by his own lust" *(James 1:14).*

Beginnings

Every day carries with it the potential for faithfulness and for failure. Every day temptation stands along the side of the path and invites us to turn aside. Knowing this, determine to be on the lookout for it, ready to refuse. Jesus will give you the power to do just that. Don't pass over this truth: We must ask of Him, in faith, what we need and He will enable us to follow Him faithfully today. So, be still. Gather your thoughts regarding what *you* need and then—ask.

We began Week 4 by talking about the two sides of temptation. Satan is the tempter and his offers seem attractive and gratifying, but once accepted turn foul. Returning to the analogy of gates, those places where entrance may be gained into our lives, he knows the access points that are common to people (usually these are the triple dangers of money, sex, and power), as well as those that are unique to us individually (some specific area of your life where you have been personally vulnerable). He watches for distraction, fatigue, and weakness, and then comes at that point of entrance to see if he can get in with a tempting offer. As bad as this is, the actual situation is far worse because of another hidden dynamic: There is already a traitor on the inside.

Turn to today's focal passage, James 1:14–15. Where is the other point of origination for sin? _____

Yes, it comes from the inside, from our own lust—those desires to have what we shouldn't. Ideally, this traitor should be rooted out and removed. But unfortunately for us, that can't happen just yet. While on this earth we live in an earthly body that will have lurking in it these desires and lusts of the mind and of the flesh. If we give attention to them, what will happen? (James 1:15) _____

_____

When the desire is formed into a plan of action to satisfy it, the actual completion of the act is far more difficult to derail. Each of us has known the experience of being rescued from the precipice of a disastrous act, from the very moment of danger. We can thank God for this. But our mothers were right: we shouldn't play in the street. We don't flirt with danger by allowing our minds to fantasize the illicit. More often than not when we allow desire to conceive, it will eventually birth the sinful act. Even if it doesn't, we need to remember that Jesus made it very clear that the mental conceiving of some acts is sin itself (Matthew 5:28).

In 2005, the emcee of a hit TV reality show told contestants that sex had cost him a lot of money (an apparent reference to his infidelity and subsequent expensive divorces). What he doesn't realize is that the cost of his lust is immeasurably beyond just money. Look to James 1:15. When sin is consummated, what does it issue in? _____ Death is always the devil's ultimate design.

Certainly a gate allows access, but more correctly it allows transit. When we allow our own lusts to intertwine with the enemy's tempting efforts, we leave the safety of our home in the city of God and go outside the walls. There we expect to have the glamorous and thrilling experience of "dancing with the stars," only to discover that we actually are dancing with the devil. And when morning comes, we're left to slink back home, degraded and ashamed.

So proactive, alert defense is the key to victory at this point. What was the shield that Paul said was our ultimate defense? (Ephesians 6:16) _____

Yes, it is faith.

To the Thessalonians (1 Thessalonians 2:18 to 3:5) Paul expressed his growing alarm for them. Satan was thwarting the teams' efforts to come and strengthen them. Severe affliction and suffering was creating

Week 6 Day 3

an environment where the believers would be more vulnerable to temptation. What did Paul send Timothy to check on? (1 Thessalonians 3:5) _____

Yes, it is their faith.

So here is the victorious action for us as we keep walking this walk. Keep trusting Jesus.

Do not let your faith fail. And look out for others. Encourage. Exhort. Pray for. He will not fail us.

Through the Day

Confess your faith in Christ. And if your faith seems weak today, confess it to Him and echo the prayer of the desperate father of the demon-possessed boy (Mark 9:24), *"I do believe; help my unbelief."* Jesus will.

Be on guard for areas where you may find yourself thinking about sin. At the moment you recognize the thoughts, reject them, firm in your faith, and begin to speak words of praise to our Savior.

Evening Reflections

Note where today you found temptation.

How did you respond?

Was there a struggle to stand and resist in faith?

Our Way—Prayer

"Lord, it is so hard. It has been so complex. Thank You that I am seeing hope and help in You. Thank You for revealing to me the vulnerable points in my life and the tempting dangers from outside and from inside. All praise to You. It felt so good to know victory. You are the victor. I praise You. And I rest in You this night. Hallelujah."

Week 6: Day 4

Hardness of Heart

Our Weapon—His Word

(Read aloud.)

"If I have forgiven anything, I did it for your sakes in the presence of Christ, so that no advantage be taken of us by Satan" *(2 Corinthians 2:10–11).*

Beginnings

Just because we do not see the enemy absolutely does not mean that he's not waiting for an opportunity. Today and tomorrow we open our lives to major areas where too often the enemy finds fertile ground. Knowing this, humble yourself before Jesus this morning. Invite Him to shine the searchlight of His love into your heart and declare to Him your desire for freedom at these points. Praise Him that He is the Lord of liberty and life.

In the 1970s, during my first year of seminary, one of my first faculty friends, Dr. Cal Guy, introduced me to a retired missionary named Bertha Smith. Miss Bertha, as she was known, was in her late 80s at that point and had served for four decades as a missionary among the Chinese. She had been part of God's glorious movement called the Shantung Revival. Even though she seemed at first to be an unlikely candidate, she was being used mightily of God to bring revival among ministers and leaders. She was gracious and spirit-filled but she was also blunt. Normally guest speakers at the seminary were picked up at the airport by students; but Cal Guy, who had Miss Bertha come and speak in his classes every semester, always picked her up himself. The first thing she would say when she got in his car was, "Cal Guy, are your sins confessed up-to-date?"

Why was this of first importance to Miss Bertha? Because she understood from painful experience and deep knowledge of God the critical importance of Paul's exhortation "Give the enemy no opportunity" (1 Timothy 5:14 NIV). When we transfer our allegiance from ourselves to our Savior, His purposes and His ways become ours.

Did Jesus forgive those who sinned against Him? (Luke 23:34) _____ When? _____

What about Stephen? (Acts 7:60) _____ When? _____

How are we to forgive? (Ephesians 4:32) _____

_____

Jesus commands us to forgive. When we don't, it is sin. What happens when we harden our hearts and refuse to repent of this? (Psalm 32:3–4) _____

What happens when we do repent? (Psalm 32:5) _____

Repentance generally, and forgiveness specifically, keep our lives intimately connected with His life. We forgive based not only on repentance by the offending party, we forgive based on Christ's forgiveness. We forgive because we are forgiven. The old separation between us and God is gone. Only sin can put distance between us. In fact Jesus told us that unforgiveness toward another blocks God's forgiveness toward us (Mark 11:25–26).

In recent months I have been walking with and praying for a friend who was twice deeply wounded by some who turned on him, maligned him, and drove him out. He told me, "I've had to go back and forgive those people a number of times just to be sure that I really have forgiven." Regardless of what was done to him, he doesn't want the injury to result in his being estranged from God. We are also making sure that the pain from injury is not confused with the pain of unforgiveness. They are not the same.

Open your Bible to today's focus verse. Who did Paul say he didn't want the enemy to take advantage of? _____ That's right. Us. With this statement we come to understand that not only does unforgiveness open the gate to Satan's entrance and activity in our own lives, it does the same in other's lives. In this passage Paul referred to a man in the Corinthian church who was living in sin (1 Corinthians 5). The church had been reluctant to deal with the man, but at Paul's urging they finally did and gloriously the man had repented. Now in his follow-up instruction (1 Corinthians 5:7) we see a clear example of how unforgiveness could give the enemy opportunity in another's life.

What does Paul instruct the church to do? (2 Corinthians 2:7)

_____

Yes, they must now comfort the man and receive him back into their fellowship. If they don't, the man could be "overwhelmed" and dangerously vulnerable to the enemy's suggestion, even possibly to his ultimate goal, death, in this case through suicide.

Forgive that you may be forgiven and that the enemy gain no advantage in you or others. Christians of old referred to this as "keeping short accounts." They knew what they were talking about.

Through the Day

If Jesus has answered your prayer of a few minutes ago by revealing an area of unforgiveness in your life, respond right now by stating your determination to forgive and asking His help to do it and mean it.

Evening Reflections

How did Christ speak to you personally today regarding this critical area of spiritual warfare—forgiveness?

Were you able to forgive?

Don't allow the enemy an advantage by putting the Lord's illumining aside. Persevere until you truly have forgiven.

Our Way—Prayer

"Savior, Your salvation is too wonderful for words, but sometimes it is also too painful. I know You know what I've suffered. Help me to forgive. I want to. I need You. Thank You for forgiving me."

Our Weapon—His Word

(Read aloud.)

"For from days of old they have not heard or perceived by ear, nor has the eye seen a God besides You, who acts in behalf of the one who waits for Him" (Isaiah 64:4).

Beginnings

Center your life this morning with this thought: Jesus is trustworthy. Today the cares of the world will, no doubt, seek to rattle you, to even sweep you off your feet.

Pray, "Lord Jesus, You are the Prince of Peace. I place my trust in You today because You know what I am facing, You care for me, and I have the promise that all my needs will be met in You. That is wonderful and I'm going to focus on that reality today. Amen."

Common a few years ago was a refrigerator magnet with the prayer: "Lord, give me patience. And I want it right now!"

It always seemed to bring a chuckle, but now I rarely see it. Could it be that the Holy Spirit convicted believers that such a prayer was actually detrimental to spiritual growth? Honestly I hope so.

I mentioned last week that choice was at the top of Americans' values list. I didn't mention that at the time of that study, the next value in importance was time. Americans don't want to wait; and as globalization advances, other cultures don't want to wait either. This is now one of those areas where cultural winds blow counter to the wind of the Spirit and thus open up an area of vulnerability for us.

Read again today's focus verse. Looking back across the span of history, Isaiah is able to declare that God *is* faithful. He is. You declare it now too. With that truth central in our minds, let's look at what Jesus says to us about anxiety (and its traveling companion, impatience) and discover the central issue that sets us free from these debilitating choices. Read Matthew 6:25.

Here Jesus tells us unequivocally, *"Do not be anxious"* (Matthew 6:25 RSV). He declares this based on a previously stated reason. What is that reason? _____

Yes. You can't love God and love money. What we love, we live for. And this is interesting. Do you know what the word translated here "anxious" actually means? It means to be pulled in different directions. When we dishonor God and live from a divided mind and heart, a tug-of-war goes on that feels like we are being pulled apart. And the reason it feels this way is because we are.

Now read on through Matthew 6:32. Worrying about how we look and how long we live and how well we eat is self-defeating. Contrary to popular thinking and the enemy's lies, it does not result in a better life. It results in an anxious, tormented, and often bitter life. The Prince of Peace came to bring peace between us and God and He wants to bring peace in our troubled hearts each moment of each day. Why, then, do we so often have no peace?

Reread Matthew 6:30. Here Jesus reveals the heart of this matter. And what is it? _____

Yes, simply, it is faith.

We live on a lake in New England. Normally the lake is frozen all winter, but the global warming of recent years has brought a new concern. Instead of heading right out onto the lake to skate or ice fish, people now are hesitant. Why? Because they don't *know* that the ice will hold them. Why don't we head right out into our daily world, following God with confidence? For the

What we love, we live for.

same reason. We don't *know* Him and so we are hesitant. We worry. We try to meet our own needs. When things don't go as we want them to, we get impatient. We push and the enemy delights to feed this downward spiral. The result? Our lives, which should be vessels of honor, are instead filled with anxiety and unhappiness. But, praise the

Lord. He has not left us hopeless in this situation. Here, simply, is what we must do.

Refocus our lives, singularly, on Him. He's already promised to take care of all the other details and needs in our lives (Matthew 6:33).

Pray. Instead of anxiety, make petition our activity. He promises peace in return (Philippians 4:6).

And be patient. He not only knows, He loves. He does everything according to His master plan which, at its heart, is a plan fueled by incredible love. When you waver, strengthen your heart to trust Him and wait on Him (James 5:8). The best way to do this is to read His Word and keep it fresh in our minds. His Spirit will cause it to guard our minds and our hearts and repulse the enemy any time he tries a scheme to disturb our trust.

Remember: Desires and demands result in anxiety and impatience. When we wait on Him, we open the door for His blessing. When we don't, we open the door for the enemy's activity. So . . .

"Resist him, firm in your faith, knowing that the same experiences of suffering are being accomplished by your brethren who are in the world. After you have suffered for a little while, the God of all grace, who called you to His eternal glory in Christ, will Himself perfect, confirm, strengthen and establish you" (1 Peter 5:9–10).

Through the Day

Have you been anxious about something? Determine to trust Him today. Remember Jesus's words: *"It shall be done to you according to your faith"* (Matthew 9:29). Note the issue here. Then in prayer, give it to Him and take His promise of Philippians 4:6–7 to heart.

Evening Reflections

Where did you recognize anxiety creeping in today? What about impatience?

Did you respond by committing it in prayer to the Lord?

Our Way—Prayer

"Lord Jesus, I know how prone I am to worry. Thank You for assuring my heart today that I can trust You. Forgive me for my impatience. You do all things well. I rest in Your perfect and wise ways and thank You for giving me peace. All praise to Your name. Amen."

Week 6 Day 5

Facilitator's Guide

Thank you for agreeing to be a facilitator. A couple of things probably have happened for you to have done that.

1. You have a spirit that is alert enough that when you read the early mention of this facilitator's guide, it sparked an interest that resulted in your turning to this page and beginning to read. Thanks.
2. You have already allowed God to work deep enough in your life that your first thought is not just "What is in this for me?" but also "What may be in this for others through me?"

That you are reading these words is an encouragement to me; it tells me that you are open to allowing God to use you to help a group of your Christian friends walk through this *Strong Walk* experience together. You may feel—quite reasonably—that you are too busy. We all feel that way. Perhaps you either have some things in your life that need to go, or there is at least one activity that was from God that now needs to be laid aside so He can use you in a new way—to facilitate this transformational experience.

I suspect that you've already taught enough to know that the teacher always benefits more from a class than do any of the students. That will likely hold true this time, but the teacher/student model should not be superimposed over this experience. This group already has a teacher. He's not only a great Teacher, He's *the* good Teacher. Good in His total character and good in His teaching methods. The teacher role for this experience is already filled—by Jesus. That's why this is not called a teacher's guide or a leader's guide. He doesn't need one.

Jesus does, however, need an assistant that I'm calling a facilitator. The reason for this is found in the meaning of the word. To *facilitate* means to prepare for, to make easier. Jesus, by His Holy Spirit, will do the teaching and the transforming. He needs someone to labor together with Him to make preparation, to get things and lives ready for that teaching. As you ask Him if He wants you to receive the gift of this responsibility, be sure you also confess to Him your willingness. If you're not willing, ask Him to work with you at that point.

As you prayerfully consider taking this responsibility, be open to sharing it with one or more people. Facilitation can be shared with the whole group, a different person taking responsibility each week. There are benefits to doing this. It probably wouldn't be my first choice, though, because of the possibility of disjointedness and varying degrees of preparedness. An individual or a pair seems to be best. This could be a married couple or two people who have served together successfully on previous projects. We have two friends who are different in just about every way and yet together are an amazingly effective team. (Yes, Kitty and Claire, I'm talking about you.) It is a beautiful thing to watch as they bring their deep friendship and complementary gifts to a task and see God pleased as He blesses their efforts to His ends. It might be that God has already prepared someone to join you in this task. Ask Him if He has.

Trust that God has brought you to this responsibility. Walk in that assurance as you draw the group together and make arrangements for their pilgrimage through this study. Recognize that the enemy doesn't want you to help God's people advance in their understanding of his ways and to walk and war against him with growing success. He will be actively opposing your service. If you team with someone to facilitate this, try to meet weekly with your partner to share what you are experiencing and to strengthen one another through prayer and encouragement.

The Group

This study is ideal for those who have walked through the *Follow Me* experience, become lifestyle prayerwalkers, and, as such, have experienced the sometimes puzzling, always painful reality of an enemy who opposes their walking with God for His kingdom purposes. If you have a group that is interested in the study but hasn't yet allowed God to speak to them about His desire for them to walk with Him in prayer, overview the *Follow Me* study. Then, together, ask God to show you His desire regarding taking this step first.

The Structure

An ideal scenario would be for group members to work through the daily material first thing in the morning, Monday through Friday, and then gather on the weekend to discuss, pray together, and integrate the truths more fully into their lives.

If you normally meet for Sunday School or small-group Bible study on Sunday morning, that one-hour time frame will work fine. If you have more flexibility, an hour and a half is better; it gives more time for discussion and for prayer for one another. You will likely find that one of the curses of our age will begin to assert itself rather quickly: information for information's sake rather than for change's sake. More time with more intentionality will help to overcome this. Remember, this is not just to learn about spiritual warfare but to welcome God's work of molding us into more biblical, and thus more effective, spiritual warriors.

It is critical to remember that this very process is a battle. As facilitator, you will carry a heavier load and will need prayer for yourself. Call or get together with your personal intercessors. Share the task to which God is calling you and ask their daily intercession for you as you facilitate this group.

Beginnings

Lay a foundation for the study to ensure a consistent start for the group. If possible, give the books out and ask everyone to read only the introduction in preparation for a launch gathering. This gathering might be a dinner party or a more informal gathering to discuss the basics from the introduction and lay out the framework for the study. If you have not set a meeting time, work out a schedule with the group. Build in ample time to pray for everyone by name. Invite the Lord to guide each one as you walk with Him as He continues His transforming work in you.

Some Alerts

Keeping the group *on topic* may be a challenge. The enemy always wants to get us off on tangents. Watch for this and be ready with a question that points back to the center of that week's study.

Keeping the group *on task* may be a challenge. Starting well isn't all that rare, but finishing well is. By the second week you will likely see some people making excuses for slighting their daily study. Be proactive, highlighting this danger in advance and encouraging and interceding for everyone at this danger point.

Keeping the group *on track* may be a challenge. It would be rare if over the course of six weeks there were not reasons for people to consider dropping out or delaying completion. Again, alert everyone in advance to this very real possibility and agree to unite in prayer that you may walk the whole path together.

Finally, remember that God knows all of this in advance. He intends to actually use the unique characteristics of your group and the events that He, as a sovereign God, brings into this period of shared pilgrimage to accomplish His purposes. He will help you stand together against the enemy while He builds the truths and the techniques of this experience deep enough into your life that you will not fall back into the old ways of thinking and living. Keep before the group the central intent—that you come out of this experience different than you went in. He is the Master Potter and He desires to shape us into vessels of honor and blessing. Don't resist Him. Let Him have His way.

Week 1: Our Reigning King, Jesus

Gather and Pray

Gathering and starting on time will be one of your first challenges. Depending on the cultural backgrounds of your group, this may vary in its difficulty. If your weekly group time is hemmed in by other scheduled activity (such as regular Sunday morning church activities), you will have to be disciplined and proactive if you are to protect the limited amount of time available and optimize the group dynamic. If your setting is more casual and the schedule more flexible, then fellowship and front-end flexibility are acceptable as long as you know the *real* time you need to start. Keep in mind that the weekly group time is important to clarify and anchor that week's key truths. This is when and how you will address the kinds of enemy activity that group members will face, and to pray for and support one another during this time.

Now for this first week's time. Once everyone is quieted, lead in a focused prayer, exalting Christ, declaring His victory, and enjoining His presence during this time and throughout the entire experience.

Review and Respond

If you have a marker board, write this week's key Scripture on the board and refer to it. Remind the group that during this past week they learned that the key to victorious spiritual warfare in daily life has two sides:

1. Christ and His infinite strength and power
2. Our living in and operating from His strength and power

State that often studies or discussions of spiritual warfare begin and revolve around Satan and his activities. Then ask: Why does this study begin with Jesus?

Allow the group members to answer.

Ask them to restate the ultimate purposes of God and of Satan as highlighted on Day 1. Allow them to respond. God's purposes are always good. Satan's never are.

Introduce the element of perception. Does it ever seem that what Satan offers is good and what God offers is bad? Ask for some examples.

Discuss perception and its power to distort and distract. What brings clarity to false perceptions? (Truth) Ask: How does God's truth do this?

Now remind the group of the tightrope walker tale. What stood out to them about this story? Make plain: It's one thing to say we believe. It's quite another to act on that belief. In the Christian life, and especially in the area of spiritual warfare, we have to actually place ourselves completely in Jesus's care and live out that trust to be victorious in the real world challenges we face.

Ask the group to share one or two examples of this.

Regardless of how things seem, who reigns over all? Yes, the Bible is unequivocal. Jesus does.

And for whom or to what end has everything been placed under Christ's authority? (Day 3) Reiterate that the way things are often perceived—that the world is at the center of everything and the church is on the periphery—is actually 180 degrees out of sync with reality. It is the church that is at the center of everything. And the church is the only entity that has the truth and the supernatural power to spread it. Elements of real truth may be found in other organizations because all real truth is from God, but the church has been made the recipient of *the* truth, the gospel. This gospel is the power of God to set all free who believe it and live it.

Ask: Does being "in Christ" mean that hurt and pain are a thing of the past? No. What does it mean? (Day 4) It means that "in Him" nothing from the enemy can come to us that has not first been permitted through by our Savior. And "in Him" we have everything we need to stand firm and faithful, walking through the trial victoriously.

Lastly, turn to John 15 and discuss the ramifications of Jesus's description of our lives as branches. Connect this with the truth in the introduction that life is a walk and that He is the One who calls and makes it possible for us to come back to the kind of walk that we were created for in the beginning.

Ask the group: How have you tried to live as a branch out there on your own? What was it like?

Now ask the group to think back on the days of this week: How did you actually do in living out the truths that we studied? (They can look back at their notes to refresh their memories.)

Ask: Was it hard to practice the discipline of setting aside a few minutes at the end of each evening to reflect back on the day? What is the advantage in doing this?

Ask them to share some of the reflections they had and how they struggled with responding as Jesus wanted them to.

Closing

Reiterate who Jesus is as reflected in our study together this week. (He is our omnipotent, victorious, and reigning Savior. He indwells and enables us to walk victoriously through this hostile world.) The walk that is centered in and anchored on Jesus is the kind of walk that truly does keep the enemy on the run.

As you prepare to lead the group in prayer, mention the central importance of the Book of Ephesians and that we will be studying the critical chapter 6 passage in this next week, learning of Christ's provisions for us and how practically to use them.

Now lead into a time of prayer. If you know the group and are assured that they are comfortable in praying out loud, ask them to pray for one another, based on what the various members have shared. If some members are not comfortable in praying out loud, call on one or two members who you know are willing and able to pray for the group. Close the time by thanking God for His saving love given in Jesus and the victory that is now ours in Him. Pray specifically for His protection of all in the group and their families and ask Him to continue to clearly and powerfully lead each member in following Him.

Week 2: Our Equipment

Gather and Pray

Settle the group—on time—and begin to prepare them to pray. When everyone is beginning to focus on the purpose for gathering, begin by reading portions of Scripture that bring our focus to God and His greatness while reminding us of His ways and character. Psalm 103 is a good example. Using this text you can focus the group's attention on the Lord by reading verses 1–2, bringing glory to His name.

Then read verses 17–19, reminding the group of God's enduring love and kindness to those who revere Him. Emphasize that this promise is to those who nurture their walk with Him (*"to those who keep His covenant"*) and who live as He intends us to (*"and who remember His precepts to do them"*). Anchor this time with the unequivocal and assuring truth of verse 19 (*"The Lord has established His throne in the heavens, and His sovereignty rules over all."*). Bow and lead the group in prayer.

As you pray, incorporate the truths of the Scripture that you have just read and then, taking this week's key Scripture (Ephesians 6:11), paraphrase its content as you lead the group in prayer. An example: "Thank You, Lord, that not only have You provided everything we need to be equipped for the warfare that this life entails, but when we are careful and consistent in keeping each piece in place, we *are* enabled to stand firm against the evil plots and plans of the enemy."

Also, keep in mind that there may be personal needs that arise with the group. Be sure and pray together for pressing needs. Otherwise, keep the focus of your prayer and your time on the study.

Review and Respond

Remind the group that as we consider our God-given equipment for spiritual warfare, our greatest asset is Jesus's already completed victory over sin, death, and the devil. That ensures ultimate victory while also providing the potential for practical victory in our daily battles.

With that glorious foundation reiterated, begin to consider the pieces of equipment that God has given us to prepare ourselves for battle. The primary purpose in this week's group time is:

1. to see everyone move beyond a superficial knowledge of the components of this "armor" to an understanding of what God is actually talking about. The metaphors (such as the breastplate or the helmet) are not the equipment. Righteousness and faith and salvation and the others are.
2. to grasp how to actually appropriate and use these real pieces of equipment.

Most of us probably wish that they were actual articles that were put on because we already know how to do that.

Ask: What are some protective items that we regularly put on?

Some examples: If we're going out into the sun, we put on sunscreen and a hat. A daughter going out bike riding puts on a helmet. A son heading out to skateboard adds elbow and knee pads to the obligatory helmet. And if we're getting into the car to drive, we put on a seat belt.

Ask: Why are these easily understood and done?

What, though, is likely the greatest danger to us?

The greatest danger we will face most days will be from our terrible enemy and his minions, yet we either go out without thought to protection or we recite a simple formula of armor inventory and then go forth hoping it worked.

Using a marker board or flip chart, ask the group to list the five defensive pieces of our God-given armor. Write them in a vertical list on the board as they are named. Don't write the corresponding metaphor (i.e., the helmet, shield, etc.). Write the actual equipment piece. The list will be truth, righteousness, peace (from the gospel), faith, and salvation.

Now take them one by one and talk about what they are, how they are used, and some personal examples of each.

More questions are provided than you will have time to ask and discuss. Select the ones you believe are most important for your group.

Limit the number of participant responses. You want to give balanced time to each of the elements. Particularly don't short the last two, prayer and the Word of God.

Truth

What is this? (It is what God says and what He says is true.) It provides a reliable baseline to live life by and measure new so-called truth against.
How is truth under attack in our world today? Discuss ways.
How does the enemy use this to attack us personally? Discuss ways members have experienced this.

Encourage members to share how they have practically encircled their lives with God's truth and faced challenges at this point.

An illustration. As I write, the Catholic Church in Massachusetts has just faced a major decision. Based on God's truth, the Catholic Church believes that God intends marriage to be between a man and woman. The state of Massachusetts disagrees and believes that marriage can also be between two people of the same sex. Biblical doctrine has been challenged by secular doctrine. The specific implication? Will the Catholic Church, through the adoption arm of its Catholic Charities, agree to begin placing orphans with same-sex couples? The decision? The Catholic bishops announced that Catholic Charities would be shut down rather than allow secular doctrine to supersede biblical doctrine.

Righteousness

What is this? (purity, goodness)
From whom do we get it? (Jesus)
How do we receive His righteousness? (by placing our faith in Him)
How do we keep our heart protected (like a bulletproof vest) by His righteousness? (Consciously remember it, confess it, and live consistent with it. This is allowing His life to transform our lives and thus denying the enemy any opportunity.)
How were you confronted or tempted by the enemy to compromise this week? How did you resist?

Peace

What is this? (We are no longer at odds with God. We are readied for battle rather than the victim of battle.)

How do we continue to walk in this peace? (We make sure that we don't revert to the self-willed life and bring strife back into the relationship, thus giving opportunity to the enemy.)

Where has this peace brought victory to your life and protection from the enemy's old avenues of success?

Faith

What is this? (trust in, and specifically, active, risking, trust in God)

What metaphor does Paul use to show how it protects us from the enemy's efforts? (a shield) Where was your trust in God challenged this week? Could you see that the enemy was behind it?

How did you respond? Did God send help, encouragement? What?

Salvation

What is this? (Classically, this is being saved from harm and destruction.) Remembering that the helmet is used to represent this, what does it protect? (our head, the center of thought and consideration) Did Satan try to sow doubts in your mind this week?

Remember: We are loved by God with an everlasting love. We are accepted.

Now going back to the board, ask the group to name the other two provisions that God has made for us to complete His provisions for us.

Write *Prayer* and *Word of God*.

What is the one offensive weapon that God has given us? (His Word) How did Jesus use the Word of God during His extended attack from the devil?

What is the critical aspect of this? (knowing God's Word so that the enemy can't distort it and the Holy Spirit can rightly apply it)

And lastly, prayer—*the* way that God intends for us to wage and win spiritual warfare. It is by prayer that we appropriate all that we need at every point of need in the ongoing battle with the enemy. We are to pray at all times in the Spirit.

Closing

As we close, let's all thank God for His complete provisions for us to walk with Him through this world. (Let each one pray as he or she is comfortable.)

Sum up thanksgiving to God and ask His protection and blessings as we begin this week to learn critical specifics about our enemy, the devil.

Week 3: Our Enemy

Gather and Pray

As you settle the group and begin to focus their attention, tell them that as you bow together in prayer, you'd like for each of them who would to take one of the seven provided elements of God's equipment (truth, righteousness, peace, faith, salvation, God's Word, and prayer) and voice a prayer thanking Him for that particular provision and, if they can, what it has meant personally to them. If there are not at least seven people in your group, as you close the prayer please thank Him for the ones that weren't mentioned.

Before beginning the study, ask how everyone is doing with the daily discipline of preparation. Were there any added difficulties this past week as they studied about the enemy? Is daily faithfulness becoming an issue? Remind them of the importance of walking through the study step-by-step and praying for God's help while calling for a renewed commitment to daily prayer and preparation.

Also, mention the daily aspect of speaking aloud each day's focus Scripture. Ask for testimonies as to why this might be important. If necessary, offer them the comparison of reading a Scripture silently and then reading it aloud. When the actual words of Scripture are spoken, the mind and the whole person are more intently engaged with and by the truth than if we just silently read the words. It also serves notice to the forces of darkness that they are people of the truth and that God's truth will be on their hearts and lips. Encourage them to be faithful to do this.

Remember: Speaking the truth into a situation changes the situation.

Review and Respond

Going to the board, ask the group: What are some things that we already knew about the devil before this week? List them. What are some things that we discovered this week about him that we hadn't known? List these on the board as well.

Ask for situations where they recognized the activity of the enemy as a result of learning about him. Write these in another column.

Knowledge is a light that can open our understanding to that which, for too long, has remained obscured and thus made us vulnerable to the devil's ongoing activity.

What truths about Satan do you think he did not want you to learn this week? List.

Why?

Often truth is hard to receive because perceptions or preconceived ideas block acceptance. Ask: Do you think perceptions could block the truth that Satan is a defeated foe? Why?

What were the four major names of the enemy that we studied in Revelation 12:9?

What is something that we learned about him from each of these names? How do these help us in standing strong against his schemes?

What are some things that we learned from our study of Satan's deception of Eve in the Garden? (Know the truth. Believe God. Stay out of conversation with the devil.)

Lastly, let's remember and reanchor this truth into our lives. God is sovereign; Satan is not. When we look at the advance of evil and darkness in our world, we must confess again the truth, God is in control. What is most important is not how things seem, but how things are. Satan is defeated. Jesus is victorious. In the battle that remains He has given us everything we need to walk and war victoriously.

Closing

Focus your closing prayer on the greatness of Christ and His victory. Try to keep the devil and references to him out of our prayer. Prayer is to God. The devil is always trying to horn in. Keep him out and God in. Remember the attributes of Jesus that we studied in Week 1 and declare them again with thanksgiving.

Where there have been struggles for some group members, pray specifically for them, asking grace to help in these times and areas of need.

Week 4: Standing Firm Against Satan's Schemes: In Person

Gather and Pray

Keeping in mind what has been going on with the group over the past few weeks, adjust the focus of the opening prayertime based on experience, struggles, needs, etc. Remind members they are walking through a transformational experience together. (*Trans* means "across or throughout" and *formation* means a "process of change.") Thus this transformational pilgrimage is a "process of change throughout." Jesus is the author of this transformation and the Holy Spirit is the agent in it. Regardless of the unique specifics of the group's experience, ensure that Christ is the center of your praying, praising Him for His character and activity, particularly as it has been shown to you and the group. As you prepare during the week for this week's gathering, ask Him to guide you to an appropriate Scripture that can inform and anchor the prayer. Invite Him afresh to have His way with each person and pray for grace to surrender to His work.

Also, remember to pray on behalf of one another (as Paul enjoins in Ephesians 6:19) that God give every group member words and courage to speak the gospel to those that He brings across their path. Pray also for holy, humble boldness to speak the words of hope that only the good news of Jesus's love and salvation hold.

Week 4

Review and Respond

Begin this week's review and response time by calling attention to the segue.

Have you ever known what God wanted you to do, but chose instead to do what you wanted to do? Why?

Did you blame the devil for your action?

Who actually is responsible?

But who was at work in the situation?

Refer to Revelation 12:11. How did New Testament believers overcome the enemy? (obedience to Jesus and witness to Jesus)

Go to the board and ask the group to list the ways that we studied this week that the enemy personally schemes and works against us. (tempts, deceives, hinders, uses fortresses, and demonizes)
What stood out to you from the study of Jesus's wilderness temptation?
Which of Jesus's responses was most helpful to you personally in dealing with the temptations that you've been most susceptible to?

Reiterate that regardless of what we have faced or where we have failed, God has a plan and He is working all the elements in reference to that plan.

Now read Paul's words in 2 Corinthians 11:3.
What does the enemy do? (deceives)
Where does the wavering, the straying, happen? (in the mind)
And regardless of what we actually do, what are we led away from? (devotion to Christ in its purity and simplicity)

We must not forget: If we are not obeying Christ, then we are obeying the devil.
Have you ever been blinded by something and made a terrible mistake as a result? Discuss.
What keeps us from being blinded by Satan's lies? (Yes, it is the truth.)
What then enables us to choose the right? (Resisting the devil and trusting Jesus's goodness, which will work a work of willingness in us to do right. Remind members of John 15:5. When we trust, rest in Him as a branch, He flows His power and life into us. When we try to do it on our own strength, we fail because "apart from Me you can do nothing.")

What is a spiritual fortress or stronghold?
What does the enemy use these for? (to exert some degree of control over our lives)
How do we tear this down? (knowledge of and use of the truth)

Lastly, come to the topic of demons, their activity, and the extent of their control.

Reiterate that while demons can effectively control nonbelievers, they cannot possess believers. Instead, "demonizing" is the biblical term for the various activities of Satan's evil spirits. Ask the group for areas in life where patterns of thought have opened up a person to false understandings that resulted in a continual pattern of sin.

If appropriate, ask the group for personal examples of how Satan has deceived in the past and for periods of time had a base of operation through thoughts that were inconsistent with God's truth.

Closing

Bow together and celebrate the liberty that has come through Christ's work. Give Him praise. As appropriate, intercede for one another at the points of existing struggle.

Stand firm together against the schemes of the enemy and declare Christ's victory in your lives. Confess any known sins and then declare your willingness and intention to follow Him. Amen and Amen.

Week 4

Week 5: Standing Firm Against Satan's Schemes: In the World

Gather and Pray

Keep in mind as the group gathers that they have been living this week in the very world where the enemy plots to trip and trap them. Studying his schemes while living in the midst of them has powerful potential, both positive and negative. Be sensitive to a range of feelings such as sadness, conviction, and disappointment on one side of the issue and responses such as denial, rationalization, and apathy on the other.

To the degree that you can ascertain these in the preliminary informal conversations of the group or from conversation with individual group members during the week, structure the opening prayer focus to bring grace and truth to bear. If we are to be transformed into biblically shaped warriors, it is of critical importance that we not ignore thoughts and activities that are inconsistent with God's truth as He illumines them, but instead turn from them and allow Him to make the changes necessary. Procrastination and rationalization give the enemy a pass to continue playing on the field of our lives.

Review and Respond

Go to the board and ask the group to share some models that they recognized this week that have influence on people. Make two columns, one for negative models and one for positive ones.

Take one of the negative examples and discuss how Satan uses it to harm our lives.

Do the same with one of the positive ones, seeking to understand how it can help us grow in Christlikeness.

Now read Matthew 6:22–23 to the group. Discuss Jesus's metaphor of a lamp and the example of plugging a lamp into an outlet. What we look at, what we plug into determines what kind of light (or darkness) we stream into our lives.

Ask for a personal example.

How can we strip from the devil these opportunities to bring detriment to our lives? (Judge media content by God's standard and then choose what is right.)

Sometimes the deception is so long-running and so deeply ingrained in a life it seems impossible to be set free from. Make plain that this is where we need to ask help from other believers. Perhaps you need to pause right here and allow some to share and then pray for one another.

Now mention the discussion (in Day 3) on values ensuring that everyone understands how easy it is to live by values other than the ones we say we live by. Ask for an example.

Then turn to page 104 and review the progression when we turn from God as our ultimate life value. Give examples of how Satan is doing this very thing in America today.

Now ask the group to share examples of worldly values that the devil has offered them to validate actions that they knew were wrong. Does anyone have a personal example of allowing ambition to be perverted by Satan's offering of a wrong value to validate it? What were the consequences?

Talk about the way back from this. (repentance, return, restitution as appropriate)

Now we come to the last avenue that we will focus on in this section of Satan's activities in the world: relationships. Turn to and read Ephesians 6:12*a*. People may seem to be the problem, but who is our struggle really with? This is a spiritual struggle in a contested, conflicted world and Satan is found to be the root of it all.

What does God want us to do? (Hebrews 12:14)

And if the person doesn't want peace, what are we to do? (Romans 12:18)

Conclude by asking everyone to open their Bibles to Luke 6:27–28. Ask someone to read Jesus's words. Is there anything here that we don't understand? Is there anything that is difficult to do? Discuss why.

Closing

Close by remembering that this area, like the others, is an opportunity for opportunity. How we respond gives either God or the enemy opportunity for further activity. God knows best. His direction is always the right direction. Once we know that, we then must take the step and do it. Ask the group to share their struggles with any of the areas that we have studied this week and then pray for one another, confessing Christ as Lord over all of life. Ask His grace and help at these very points of need.

Week 6: Standing Firm Against Satan's Schemes: Through the Flesh

Gather and Pray

Keeping in mind that today we are coming to the end of this journey together, ask the group to express to the Lord in the opening prayer-time what the journey has meant to them personally. Be sure that you sum up their expressions with grateful thanks to Jesus for His role in every aspect of our liberty and our ongoing victory.

Review and Respond

What are some of the desires of the flesh that we see in society today? What are some that you struggle with or have struggled with in the past?

Read the focus Scripture for Day 1 (Galatians 5:16–17*a*). How do we keep from carrying out the desires of the flesh? (walk in the Spirit; i.e., submitting to His control, His power, His guidance)

A pastor friend told me of his often-repeated struggle with impure or unhealthy thoughts and how he had to both want to keep them out and persist in keeping them out. Ask group members if they have had similar experiences. How did they respond? How did God help them?

It certainly may be that group members don't feel comfortable in sharing "gates" where they have often allowed themselves to be betrayed by desires of the mind. This is understandable. Do consider pausing here to allow those who would to express in prayer thanksgiving for Christ's forgiveness and His help in these times of need.

Now we turn to the flip side of the coin called temptation. In Week 4 we saw that the devil is the tempter. This week we learned that his temptations are so dangerous because we already have a traitor living on the inside who is ready to team up with him for our demise. Ask: What is that traitor's name? (lust) What do we normally associate lust with? (sex) Actually, though, what is lust? (desire to have what we shouldn't) Ask for some examples.

So what do we do to keep the traitor, lust, from opening the gate to our lives and joining forces with the enemy? We keep faith. Paul is clear. Faith is the shield that stops the incoming efforts of the enemy and faith is the force that enables us to resist lust and all the other temptations that arise from impure desires.

We conclude our study by focusing on two areas of our lives where too often the enemy finds the gate standing open: hardness of heart and impatience of life.

How are we to forgive? (Ephesians 4:32) And when we won't, what happens? (Psalm 32:3–4)

Ask the group if anyone would share a personal example at this point.

Why is it hard to forgive? Discuss the answers.

When we refuse to forgive, what happens to our relationship with God? (tension, strain)

And the solution? (forgive)

In this area, like all others, when you need help ask. He has already promised to give it (Matthew 7:7).

Ask: Did anyone think it unusual that of all the many schemes of the devil relating to the flesh, the last one we would study would be the traveling companions, anxiety and impatience?

Why are these two so important and our carefulness regarding them so critical?

What did we learn this week was the second most important American value? (time)

What did we learn is the heart of the issue regarding uneasiness, insecurity, and impatience? (Yes, it is that we don't know God.) When we know Him, we *know* that we can trust Him. When we trust Him, we are at peace. No need to worry. No need to push.

Ask the group where they saw themselves in this last day's study. This last week's.

List those on the board.

Turn to 1 Peter 5:9–10 and ask someone to read this to the group.

"Resist him, firm in your faith, knowing that the same experiences of suffering are being accomplished by your brethren who arc in the world. After you have suffered for a little while, the

God of all grace, who called you to His eternal glory in Christ, will Himself perfect, confirm, strengthen and establish you" (1 Peter 5:9–10).

What does God tell us to do and what will He do?

Close by reading to the group this last day's focal Scripture (Isaiah 64:4).

There is no god like God. Never has there been or will there be. He *will* act on our behalf as we walk uprightly and look to Him in faith, waiting with assured expectation.

What a resistance of the devil this is. The enemy knows that this kind of walk truly does keep him on the run.

Closing

Lead the group into a closing prayertime and allow them to express thanks and praise to God for all that He is and all that He has done over these weeks of study and struggle together. All praise to Jesus. He is our salvation. He is our hope. He is our way.

May God continue to richly bless you as you daily walk strong in Christ's victory and see His kingdom extended until all the earth is a praise to His glory. Amen.

New Hope® Publishers is a division of WMU®,
an international organization that challenges Christian believers
to understand and be radically involved in God's mission.
For more information about WMU, go to www.wmu.com.
More information about New Hope books may be found
at www.newhopepublishers.com. New Hope books
may be purchased at your local bookstore.

YOU MAY Enjoy

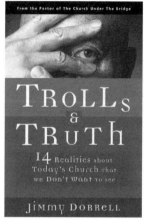

Trolls & Truth
14 Realities About Today's Church
That We Don't Want to See
Jimmy Dorrell
ISBN 1-59669-010-0

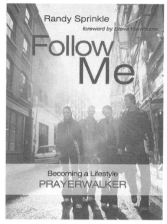

Follow Me
Becoming a Lifestyle Prayerwalker
Randy Sprinkle
ISBN 1-56309-948-9

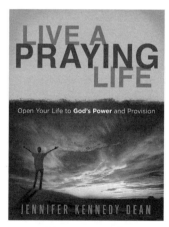

Live a Praying Life
Open Your Life to God's Power and Provision
Jennifer Kennedy Dean
ISBN 1-56309-752-4

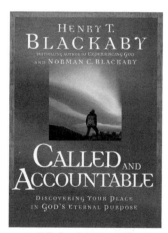

Called and Accountable
Discovering Your Place in God's Eternal Purpose
Henry T. Blackaby and Norman C. Blackaby
ISBN 1-56309-946-2

Available in bookstores everywhere

For information about these books or any New Hope product, visit **www.newhopepublishers.com**.